Quick-to-Sew
ONE-DAY GIFTS™

Edited by Beth Wheeler

HOUSE of
WHITE
BIRCHES

PUBLISHERS
SINCE 1947

Quick-to-Sew One-Day Gifts

Editor: Beth Wheeler
Design Manager: Vicki Blizzard
Product Development Manager: Jeanne Stauffer
Project Supervisor: Barb Sprunger
Technical Editor: Mary Jo Kurten
Copy Editor: Mary Nowak
Technical Artists: Leslie Brandt, Julie Catey, Jessica Rothe
Editorial Coordinator: Tanya Turner

Photography: Tammy Christian, Jeff Chilcote, Jennifer Fourman
Photography Stylist: Arlou Wittwer
Photography Assistant: Linda Quinlan

Production Coordinator: Brenda Gallmeyer
Book Cover Design: Erin Augsburger, Jessi Butler
Production Artist: Ronda Bechinski
Production Assistants: Shirley Blalock, Dana Brotherton, Marj Morgan
Traffic Coordinator: Sandra Beres

Publishers: Carl H. Muselman, Arthur K. Muselman
Chief Executive Officer: John Robinson
Marketing Director: Scott Moss
Book Marketing Manager: Craig Scott
Product Development Director: Vivian Rothe
Publishing Services Manager: Brenda R. Wendling

Printed in the United States of America
First Printing: 2000
Library of Congress Number: 99-85880
ISBN: 1-882138-60-0

A Quick Note

I love to give presents! The challenge of planning a gift and wrapping it to fit the personality and taste of someone special is a real treat for me - and the anticipation of watching her (or him) open the package is enough to turn me into an impatient child all over again.

When we give a gift to a loved one, we present them with a package that includes the item, pretty wrapping paper, bows and ribbons, and perhaps a card to complete the presentation. But, there is actually much more in that special package. It holds the gift of our time, our good wishes and a piece of ourselves!

That's why we placed so much time and planning into the design and selection of the projects in this book. When you select one to make and give as a gift, you are trusting us to help express your feelings to someone special.

We selected projects for dolls, toys, wearables for adults and children, items to decorate the home, holiday decorations and more. Most of these projects can be completed by those with average sewing skills. And most of these projects include designer touches that make them look anything but easy. We won't give away your secret about how little time they actually took to make!

I hope you enjoy browsing through this book and choosing several projects to make as gifts. Don't forget to treat yourself, too!

Sincerely,

Beth Wheeler

Editor

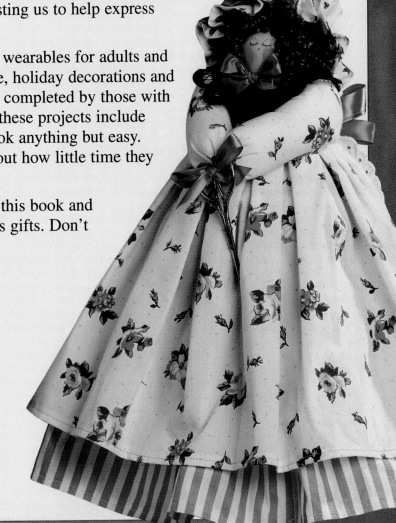

Time-Saving Treasures for the Home

Pillows and Comforts in a Jiffy

Quick-Time Kitchen Goodies

Fast and Fun Baby Gifts

It's Never Too Late for Dolls and Toys

Last-Minute Wearables

The Night Before the Christmas Gift Exchange

Time-Saving Treasures for the Home

The gifts we give to loved ones are more than just a courtesy, they are expressions of our regard for someone and what that person means to us. Select a quick-to-sew gift for the home in your friend's colors to reflect your bond and common interests.

Does your friend like to sew? The handy sewing caddy is perfect for take-along projects. Is she a pet owner? Our delightful pet pillows are sure to please. The variety of textures, materials and techniques offers something for everyone.

Sitting Kitties

Whimsical little kitties to tuck here and there for fun. Perch them on the mantel or slip them between the collectibles in your cupboard.

Project Specifications

Skill Level: Beginner
Large Kitty Size: Approximately 11" x 6"
Small Kitty Size: Approximately 8" x 5"

Materials

For Each Large Kitty
- ⅓ yard fabric
- 2 (11mm) black shank buttons
- ½ cup beans or pellets
- 20" (10mm) cording
- 3 pieces 19-gauge black craft wire each 9"–11"

For Each Small Kitty
- 10½" x 21" piece of fabric
- 2 (5mm) black shank buttons
- ¼ cup beans or pellets
- 14" (10mm) cording
- 3 pieces 19-gauge black craft wire each 8"–9"

For Both Kitties
- Polyester fiberfill
- Black 6-strand embroidery floss
- All-purpose thread to match fabrics
- 2" square fusible interfacing
- 1 yard ribbon for neck bow
- Embroidery needle
- Fabric glue (optional)
- Needle-nose pliers and wire cutters
- Basic sewing supplies and tools

Instructions

Step 1. Trace and cut kitty pieces as directed on pattern.

Step 2. Stitch through and around cording ends securely to prevent fraying (may also use a dab of fabric glue on cord ends).

Step 3. Fuse 2" square of fusible interfacing on reverse side of body front as shown on pattern. Mark nose placement.

Step 4. With 6 strands of black embroidery floss embroider muzzle line and nose. For muzzle line make a ¾" straight stitch down from the center bottom of the nose. Make satin stitches across nose as shown in Fig. 1.

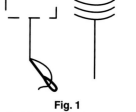

Fig. 1
Embroider nose and muzzle line.

Step 5. Place front and back pieces right sides together. Pin one end of cording to right side of body front as indicated on pattern. Pin other end of tail to front of body to keep out of the way. Pin body front and back together, making sure tail is inside. Stitch with ⅜" seam allowance, leaving bottom open and opening on one side for turning.

Step 6. Right sides together, pin gusset to bottom of kitty, matching tips of gusset to side seams of kitty. Stitch with ⅜" seam allowance and clip curves.

Step 7. Clip seam at top of head as indicated on pattern. Trim seams at tips of ears as shown in Fig. 2.

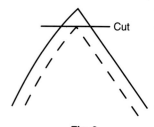

Fig. 2
Trim ears as shown.

Step 8. Turn kitty right side out. Place beans or pellets in bottom of kitty. Stuff ears with small amounts of polyester fiberfill, then fill rest of body. Slipstitch opening in body side closed.

Step 9. Coil tail around front of body as shown in photo. Tack to body with slipstitches or glue with fabric glue.

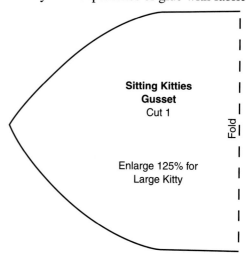

**Sitting Kitties
Gusset
Cut 1**

Fold

Enlarge 125% for
Large Kitty

Step 10. With embroidery needle and matching thread, insert needle in back of head and bring out to eye position on front. Thread button and insert needle over a few threads and return to back of head. Pull tight to indent. Repeat until secure. Repeat for second eye.

Step 11. Insert wires one at a time in

through the fabric at the side of the nose and out the other side. Center wires to nose. Use needle-nose pliers to shape whiskers as desired adding kinks and curls.

Step 12. Tie ribbon around the neck in a bow.

—By Barbara Matthiessen

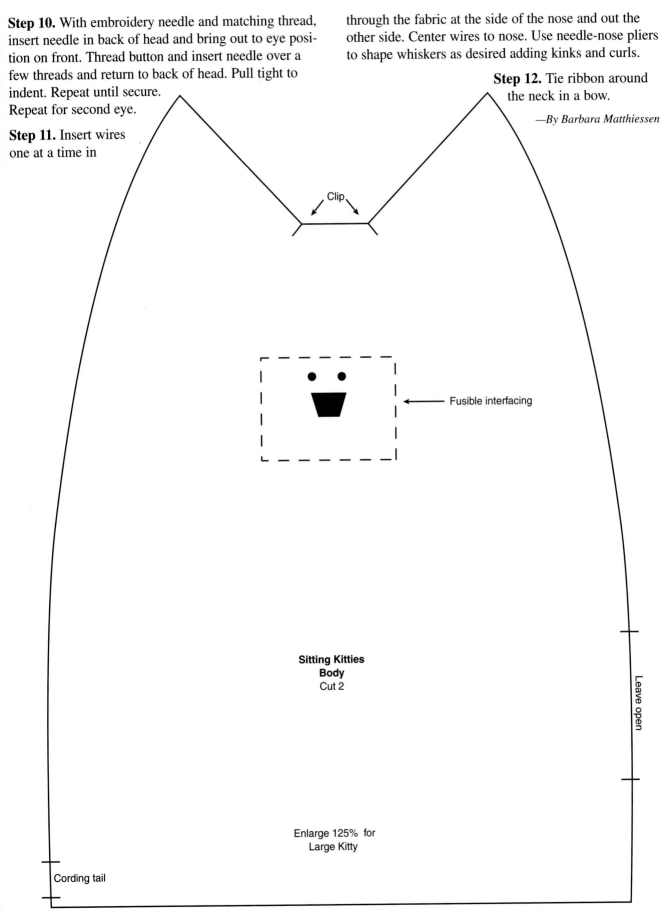

Clip

Fusible interfacing

Sitting Kitties
Body
Cut 2

Leave open

Enlarge 125% for
Large Kitty

Cording tail

Sunbonnet Sue Doorstop

Sunbonnet Sue, dressed in feedsack pastels, was a favorite in the 1930s. Dress this quick-to-make Sue in reproduction prints to brighten any room in your house.

Project Specifications

Skill Level: Beginner

Doorstop Size: Approximately 14" tall

Materials

- 1 yard pink floral print
- ½ yard pink coordinating plaid
- ¼ yard muslin
- 6" heart doily
- Polyester fiberfill
- 2 liter plastic soda bottle
- Sand or other weight product for bottle
- Low-temperature hot-glue gun and glue
- All-purpose thread to match fabrics
- ½ yard ¼"-wide ribbon for basket
- Tiny basket and small silk flowers
- Basic sewing supplies and tools

Instructions

Head and Hands

Step 1. Trace and cut head and arms as directed on pattern. Place right sides of each together and sew around leaving top of arms and lower edge of head open. Clip seams; turn right side out.

Step 2. Stuff head and arms firmly.

Clothing

Step 1. From pink floral print, cut one piece 14" x 33" for dress.

Step 2. Turn under ¼" twice and stitch one long edge of dress fabric for hem. With hand- or machine-gathering stitches gather top edge of dress piece and pull up gathering threads to fit around neck of bottle. Fold gathered fabric right sides together and sew the back seam.

Step 3. Cut sleeves as directed on pattern. Place two sleeves right sides together and sew around curved edges. Stitch ¼" hem around sleeve bottom. Turn sleeve right side out. By hand or machine, sew gathering threads 1"

above hem. Place a small amount of polyester fiberfill in each sleeve. Slip an arm into the sleeve bottom and pull the gathering threads tight. Tie off and clip threads. Tack arm into sleeve to hold. Repeat for other sleeve.

Apron

Step 1. Cut a 10" x 18" piece of pink plaid fabric to make apron, a 2½" x 5" strip to make apron band and a 2½" x 9" strip to make apron neck band.

Step 2. Turn under ¼" of apron piece twice and stitch one long edge and two short edges for hem.

Step 3. Hand-sew gathering stitches ½" from apron top. Pull gathering stitches to measure 4" across. Right sides together, place gathered area on one edge of apron band. Center so there is ½" excess on each side of band. Sew apron to band, folding side edges in. Fold top edge under ¼" and sew to back side of apron top to finish.

Step 4. Place pocket pieces right sides together and sew around leaving a 2" opening at top for turning. Clip all around and turn right side out. Press and top-stitch across top.

Sunbonnet Sue Doorstop
Apron Pocket
Cut 2 pink floral

Step 5. Fold apron neck band edges to center. Fold again and sew along long edge. Lay apron pieces aside.

Bonnet

Step 1. From pink plaid fabric cut a 16" square. Fold twice. Place pattern on folds as directed and cut.

Step 2. From pink floral fabric trace and cut bonnet brim as directed on pattern. Cut bonnet tie 3½" x 45".

Step 3. Place bonnet brim pieces right sides together and sew around curved edge. Clip seam, turn right side out and press.

Step 4. By hand or machine, sew gathering stitches around bonnet top circle. Pull up threads until circle fits head. Do not fasten or cut threads.

Step 5. Fold bonnet tie right sides together and sew on long edge, leaving a 4" opening at the center of the tie. Angle the stitching at ends of tie. Turn right side out.

Step 6. Smooth out a 4" area on the gathered circle where the gathering threads end. Fasten threads and cut. Sew the 4" area of the hat top to one side of the 4" open area on the bonnet tie. Fold the remaining side of 4" opening under ¼" and hand-stitch in place on the inside of the bonnet top.

Step 7. Pin one edge of bonnet brim to remaining gathered fabric on hat top. Sew in place. Turn other raw edge of hat brim under ¼" and hand-stitch in place to finish.

Sunbonnet Sue Doorstop
Bonnet Top
Cut 2 pink plaid on 2 folds

Sunbonnet Sue Doorstop
Bonnet Brim
Cut 2 pink floral on fold

Fold

Fold

Fold

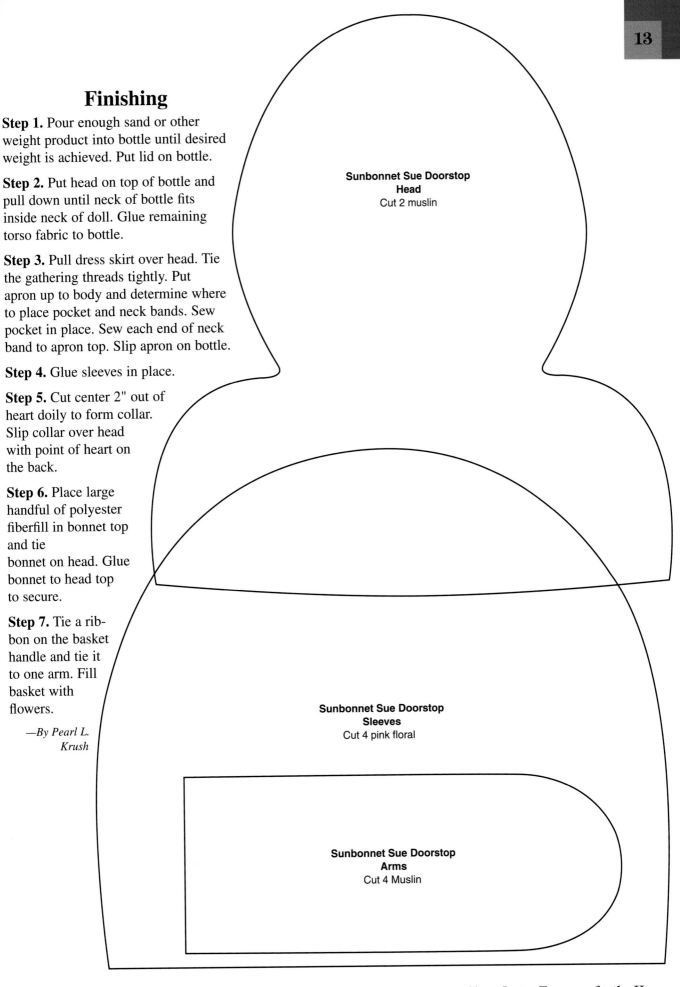

Finishing

Step 1. Pour enough sand or other weight product into bottle until desired weight is achieved. Put lid on bottle.

Step 2. Put head on top of bottle and pull down until neck of bottle fits inside neck of doll. Glue remaining torso fabric to bottle.

Step 3. Pull dress skirt over head. Tie the gathering threads tightly. Put apron up to body and determine where to place pocket and neck bands. Sew pocket in place. Sew each end of neck band to apron top. Slip apron on bottle.

Step 4. Glue sleeves in place.

Step 5. Cut center 2" out of heart doily to form collar. Slip collar over head with point of heart on the back.

Step 6. Place large handful of polyester fiberfill in bonnet top and tie bonnet on head. Glue bonnet to head top to secure.

Step 7. Tie a ribbon on the basket handle and tie it to one arm. Fill basket with flowers.

—*By Pearl L. Krush*

Sunbonnet Sue Doorstop
Head
Cut 2 muslin

Sunbonnet Sue Doorstop
Sleeves
Cut 4 pink floral

Sunbonnet Sue Doorstop
Arms
Cut 4 Muslin

Huggy Bear Draft Dodger

This adorable little bear intends to keep you warm and cozy. Stretch him out on a chilly windowsill or let him stop the cold air that sneaks under your door.

Project Specifications

Skill Level: Beginner

Draft Dodger Size: Any size

Materials

- 1 yard acrylic fur, fleece, felt or other nonwoven fabric
- Scraps of brown felt
- 2 small black buttons for eyes
- 1 medium round black button for mouth
- 1 large black oval button for nose
- Brown #3 pearl cotton or 6-strand embroidery floss
- All-purpose thread to match fabric
- Polyester fiberfill
- Pellets, buckwheat, sawdust or other dense filler
- Basic sewing supplies and tools

Instructions

Step 1. Cut two pieces of fur 7" x 36" (or desired length to fit window or door frame). Round the ends.

Step 2. Place fur pieces wrong sides together. Stitch around periphery with ¼" seam allowance, leaving an opening in the center of one side for stuffing.

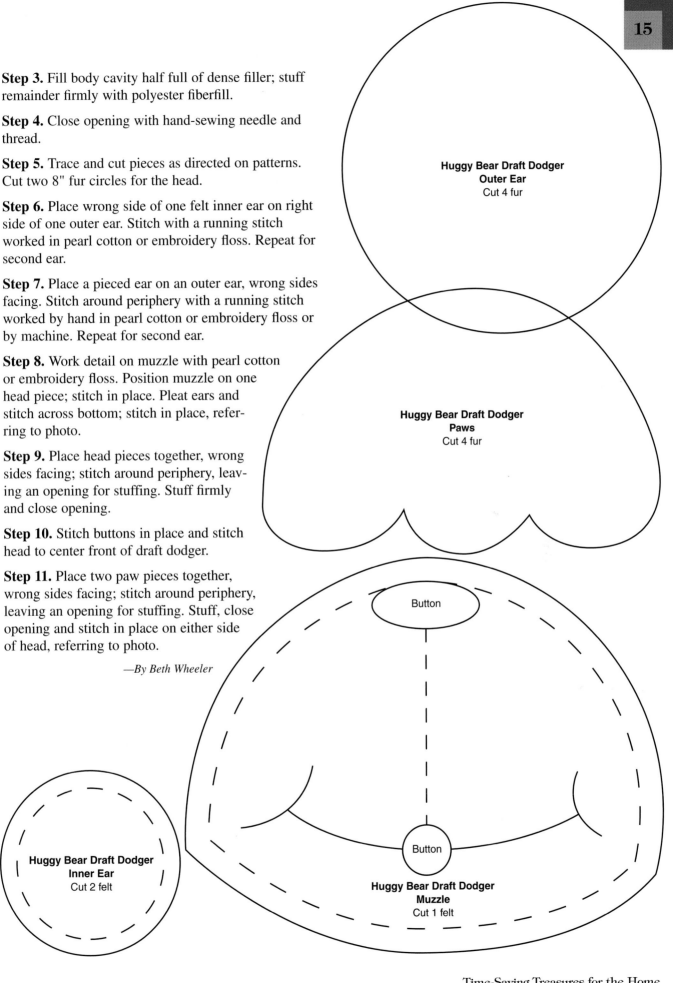

Step 3. Fill body cavity half full of dense filler; stuff remainder firmly with polyester fiberfill.

Step 4. Close opening with hand-sewing needle and thread.

Step 5. Trace and cut pieces as directed on patterns. Cut two 8" fur circles for the head.

Step 6. Place wrong side of one felt inner ear on right side of one outer ear. Stitch with a running stitch worked in pearl cotton or embroidery floss. Repeat for second ear.

Step 7. Place a pieced ear on an outer ear, wrong sides facing. Stitch around periphery with a running stitch worked by hand in pearl cotton or embroidery floss or by machine. Repeat for second ear.

Step 8. Work detail on muzzle with pearl cotton or embroidery floss. Position muzzle on one head piece; stitch in place. Pleat ears and stitch across bottom; stitch in place, referring to photo.

Step 9. Place head pieces together, wrong sides facing; stitch around periphery, leaving an opening for stuffing. Stuff firmly and close opening.

Step 10. Stitch buttons in place and stitch head to center front of draft dodger.

Step 11. Place two paw pieces together, wrong sides facing; stitch around periphery, leaving an opening for stuffing. Stuff, close opening and stitch in place on either side of head, referring to photo.

—By Beth Wheeler

Huggy Bear Draft Dodger Outer Ear Cut 4 fur

Huggy Bear Draft Dodger Paws Cut 4 fur

Button

Button

Huggy Bear Draft Dodger Inner Ear Cut 2 felt

Huggy Bear Draft Dodger Muzzle Cut 1 felt

Apple Wall Rack

*Bright plaid apples all in a row—a project you can complete in an hour,
but enjoy every day when you hang a coat, hat or purse on one of the Shaker pegs.*

Project Specifications

Skill Level: Beginner
Rack Size: 24" x 12½"

Materials

- Wool plaid scraps
- Green felt scraps
- Brown wool scraps
- 19" x 10" background fabric
- Scraps of fusible transfer web
- Tear-away stabilizer 19" x 10"
- 3 pieces batting 18" x 7"
- All-purpose thread to match fabrics
- 3 (½") red buttons
- Rack with 17" x 6" opening
- Basic sewing supplies and tools

Note: Project completed with Sudberry House, (800) 243-2607, Shaker Coat Rack item #10101.

Instructions

Step 1. Trace apple and stem shapes onto paper side of fusible transfer web; cut out leaving roughly ½" margin around shapes.

Step 2. Fuse to wrong side of plaid and brown wool fabrics; cut out on tracing line.

Step 3. Referring to photo, position pieces in order, working from background to foreground. Draw a 17" x 6" rectangle on cardboard that comes with rack and use as guide for accurate

positioning within opening. Make sure everything fits before fusing.

Step 4. Back fabric panel with stabilizer and machine-appliqué around shapes with buttonhole or satin stitch. Tear stabilizer away.

Step 5. Trace leaf patterns on green felt. Sew each leaf in place with red button.

Step 6. Pad cardboard insert with batting. Cut away excess. Center apple panel and assemble rack following manufacturer's instructions.

—By Judi Kauffman

Stem
for Apple 3

Leaf
for Apple 3

Apple 3

Apple 2

Leaf
for Apple 2

This part is under Apple 2

Apple 1

Stem
for Apple 1

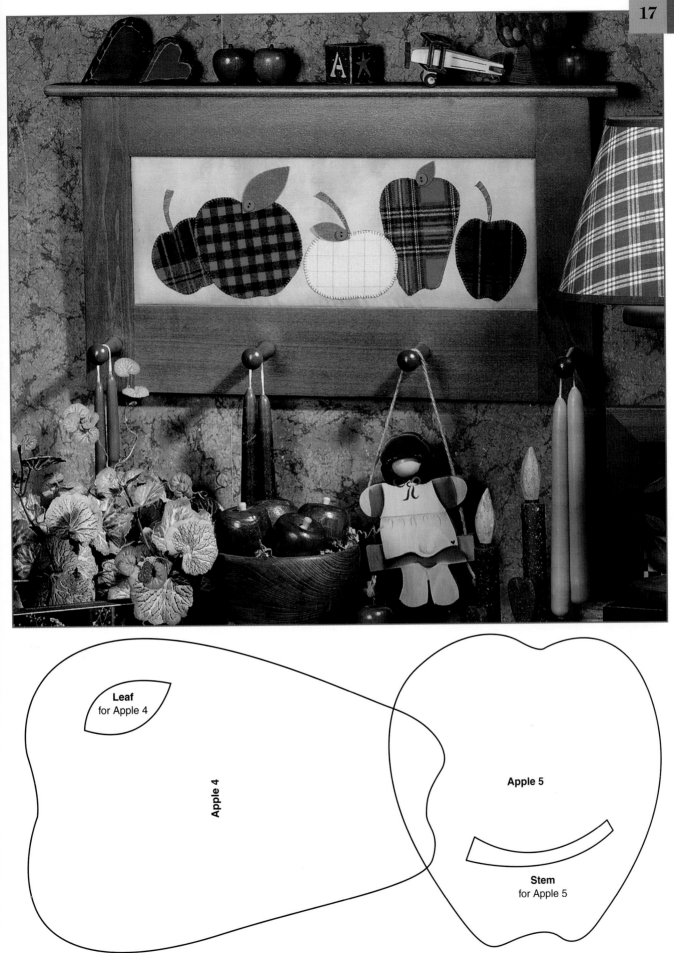

Leaf
for Apple 4

Apple 4

Apple 5

Stem
for Apple 5

Time-Saving Treasures for the Home

Chair Arm Sewing Caddy

Keep your sewing tools handy in this quick-to-make organizer. It's always ready to move when you are—from room to room, to the car or the doctor's office.

Project Specifications
Skill Level: Beginner
Caddy Size: Approximately 8" x 20"

Materials
- ½ yard tan plaid flannel
- ¼ yard tea-dyed muslin
- 2" lace doily
- 5" lace doily
- Brown 6-strand embroidery floss
- 5 small buttons
- Polyester fiberfill
- All-purpose thread to match fabrics
- ¼ yard thin batting
- Water-soluble marker
- Basic sewing supplies and tools

Instructions
Note: ¼" seams used throughout.

Step 1. Trace and cut fabrics as directed on patterns.

Step 2. Trace compartment stitching lines and words onto front pocket muslin with water-soluble marker.

Step 3. Referring to photo, stitch doilies in place.

Step 4. With 2 strands of brown embroidery floss stitch words with running stitch. Add buttons.

Step 5. Place two muslin pocket pieces wrong sides together and baste around outside edge. Cut strip of flannel 2" x 9". Place face down along top of pocket front. Stitch, then fold to back, turning raw edge under ¼". Slipstitch in place. Machine stitch along compartment lines.

Step 6. Place completed pocket on front of flannel caddy piece. Baste in place.

Step 7. Cut one muslin piece, using pattern, for pincushion. Using caddy pattern as a guide, determine placement for pincushion. Fold pincushion

piece down toward pocket and stitch across. Fold pincushion back in place. Fold remaining long edge of pincushion under ¼" and stitch to caddy. Stuff with polyester fiberfill.

Step 8. Place two flannel caddy pieces right sides together. Add batting piece on bottom. Stitch around sides and pocket, making a tuck at centers of pincushion when sewing over stuffed pocket. Leave top open. Clip seams, turn and slipstitch open end to finish.

—By Karen Mead

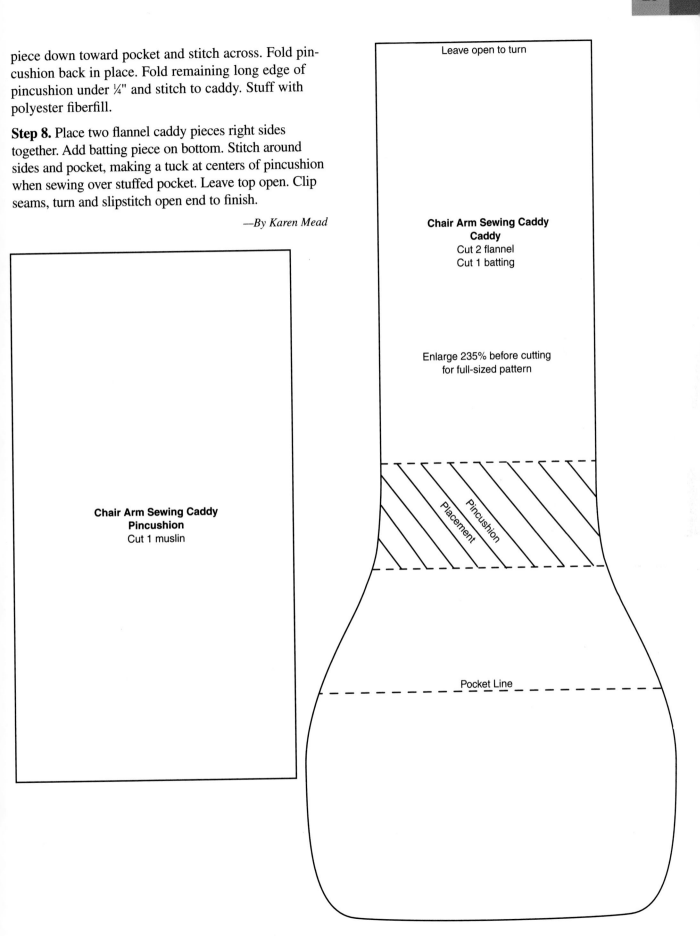

Leave open to turn

**Chair Arm Sewing Caddy
Caddy**
Cut 2 flannel
Cut 1 batting

Enlarge 235% before cutting
for full-sized pattern

Pincushion
Placement

Pocket Line

**Chair Arm Sewing Caddy
Pincushion**
Cut 1 muslin

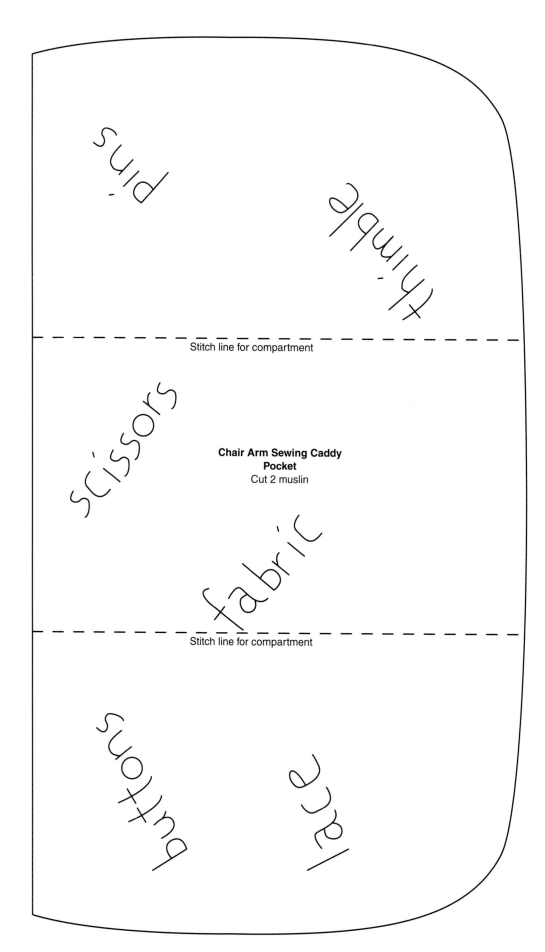

Stitch line for compartment

Chair Arm Sewing Caddy
Pocket
Cut 2 muslin

Stitch line for compartment

Floral Wall Hanging

Wooly bully is the byword for this renewed craft technique combining sewing and hooking. No edges to turn under, so expect to enjoy quick results!

Project Specifications

Skill Level: Intermediate

Wall Hanging Size: 17" x 11"

Materials

- 2 (17" x 11") pieces light pastel wool or felt for background
- Scraps of coral, rust, teal, dark blue, tan, gold and yellow-green wool or felt for appliqué and hooking
- 3 skeins olive green 6-strand embroidery floss
- Fusible transfer web (optional)
- All-purpose thread to match appliqué pieces
- Rug hook or metal crochet hook F, G or H
- Basic sewing supplies and tools

Instructions

Note: To achieve mottled appearance of background fabric in photo, wash wool with a fabric that will bleed color. The result is a pleasant, irregularly colored fabric.

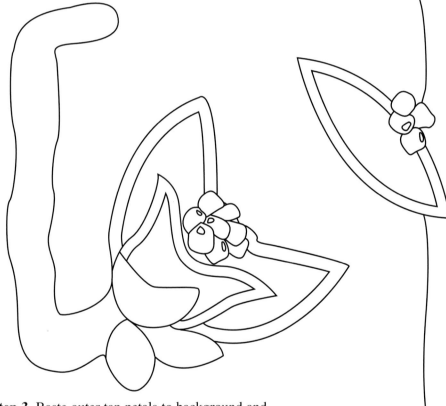

This piece has a primitive look. Precise cutting and stitching are not necessary. Irregularities in size, shape and stitching will add to its charm.

Step 1. Referring to photo, start with one coral flower. Cut and baste (or fuse) coral petals to background and machine- or hand-buttonhole stitch.

Step 2. Cut and baste tan center petal and machine-stitch to background with diamond-like pattern.

Step 3. Baste outer tan petals to background and machine-stitch with a straight stitch.

Step 4. Cut wool or felt strips for base of flower petals ⅛" by 12". Hand hook. Hooking directions are at right.

Step 5. Baste small leaves at base of flower petals and machine-stitch with straight stitch.

Step 6. Cut and baste long stems of coral flowers to background and machine-stitch full length of stem with 4 rows of straight stitching. Baste large leaves to

stems and machine-stitch.

Step 7. Follow the above procedure to complete other flowers, referring to photo.

Step 8. Cut wool or felt stems for smaller flowers ¼" x 12". Hand hook through background fabric.

Step 9. Hand hook additional decorative areas using ⅛" strips of wool or felt.

Step 10. Place finished top on backing piece. Secure the layers with 3 strands of olive green embroidery floss, worked in a high-low buttonhole stitch.

Note: If you are dissatisfied with a flower, simply stitch another on top. There are no rules when creating a piece of art. It's yours.

Hand Hooking

Step 1. With your right hand, hold the hook above the work.

Step 2. With your left hand, hold the wool strip with your thumb and index finger underneath the work.

Step 3. Insert hook through the work and pull the end of the strip to the top of the work. Leave a "tail" of about ½", which will be trimmed later.

Step 4. Insert hook again and pull a loop to the front of the work. The height of the loop should be equal to the width of the strip. Therefore, if the strip is ¼" wide, the loop should be ¼" high. Continue inserting hook and pulling loops through until desired length is achieved or you reach the end of the strip. Pull remainder of tail to the top of work. It will be trimmed later to match the rest of the pile.

Step 5. If more length is needed, repeat Step 3, pulling the "tail" of the new strip through the same hole as the one finished last. Each loop should touch, but not crush, the loop next to it.

Note: If you are not satisfied with the loops, just pull out and rehook.

—By Thaea Lloyd

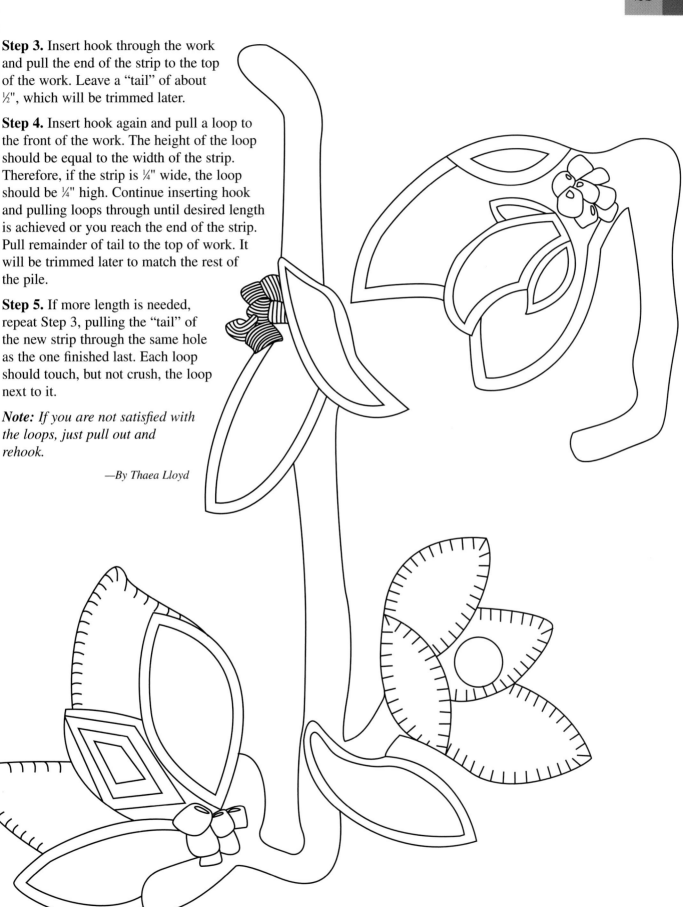

Pet Pillows

Pamper your poochie prince or kitty queen with a comfy pillow bed made soft and cozy from washable acrylic fur or fleece. Even the dog will purr!

Project Specifications

Skill Level: Beginner

Pillow Size: Approximately 28" x 30"

Materials

- ⅞ yard acrylic fur or acrylic fleece
- Pattern paper
- Natural heavy-duty thread
- 2–3 pounds polyester fiberfill
- Large coat button for fish eye (optional)
- Basic sewing supplies and tools

Instructions

Step 1. Make full-size paper pattern for pillow of choice. Pattern includes ½" seam allowance.

Step 2. Cut two pieces from fur or fleece.

Step 3. Place pieces together, right sides facing. Stitch around periphery with ½" seam allowance, leaving an opening for turning.

Step 4. Stitch again, ⅛" inside the first stitching line.

Step 5. Clip curves, trim seam allowances, and turn right side out.

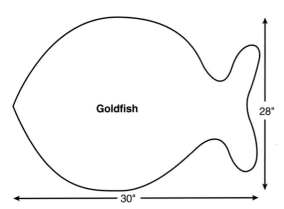

Goldfish

28"

30"

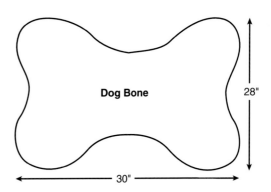

Dog Bone

28"

30"

Step 6. Stuff firmly with polyester fiberfill.

Step 7. Close opening with hand-sewing needle and doubled thread.

Step 8. If your pet won't chew it, stitch a coat button on the fish for an eye.

—By Beth Wheeler

Pillows
and
Comforts
in a Jiffy

H uggy pillows and
snuggly throws can
brighten a room and
offer respite from the hectic day.
Stitch a selection from our
cornucopia of tactile delights.
Cozy fleece, handsome tapestry,
diaphanous sheers, nubby
chenille—the fabric sets the mood
with color, texture and style.

Vintage Photo Pillow

Products for photo transfer onto fabric are widely available and offer a wonderful, unique way to preserve treasured photographs and memories for special gifts. See photo on page 26.

Project Specifications

Skill Level: Beginner
Pillow Size: 14" x 14"

Materials

- Copy of photograph or postcard 3¾" square
- Photo transfer medium
- 4¾" square fine weave smooth white fabric for photo
- ¼ yard each of four pastel print fabrics
- ½ yard coordinating print for pillow back
- 15" square low-loft cotton batting
- Metallic gold thread
- 14" pillow form
- All-purpose thread to match fabric
- Fabric stabilizer (optional)
- Basic sewing supplies and tools

Instructions

Note: Use ¼" seam allowance throughout.

Step 1. Transfer photo to white fabric square, following manufacturer's instructions.

Step 2. From each pastel print fabric cut two strips 3" x 9⁵⁄₁₆". Assign each color an identifying letter A, B, C or D.

Step 3. Using Fig. 1 as a placement guide, join pairs of strips in four blocks as shown. Press seams open. Sew blocks together leaving ¼" unsewn at center edges (where photo will be inserted later). Press seams toward outside.

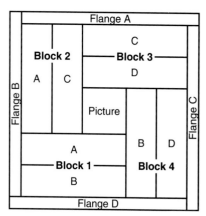

Fig. 1
Stitch strip-blocks and flanges as shown.

Step 4. Turn under and press raw edges where photo will be inserted.

Step 5. Center pillow front on batting and position photo fabric under it in center opening; pin.

Step 6. Using a decorative machine stitch and metallic gold thread, stitch through all layers along seam lines.

Step 7. From each pastel fabric cut two strips 1¼" x 14¾" for pillow flanges. Add one strip to each side of pillow front following color guide in Fig. 1. Stop stitching ¼" from end of each seam in order to add next flange.

Step 8. Using decorative machine stitch and metallic gold thread, stitch only the short-end seams as shown in Fig. 2.

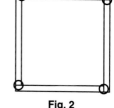

Fig. 2
Stitch only the short-end seams of each flange.

Step 9. Cut two 14" x 11¾" pieces for pillow back. Turn under 1" of one long edge of each piece and then turn under 1" again for hem. Use a decorative stitch along edges if desired (may need stabilizer).

Step 10. Overlap hemmed edges of pillow backs at center to make 14" square as shown in Fig. 3; pin. Stitch pillow flanges same as front referring to Step 7.

Step 11. Right sides together, stitch pillow front to pillow back. Batting should be just small enough not to get caught in seam. Turn right side out; press.

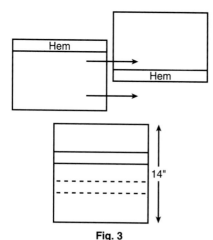

Fig. 3
Overlap pillow back pieces to make 14" square.

Step 12. With decorative thread in needle and bobbin, stitch around entire flange seam through front and back. Insert pillow.

—By Cindy Gorder

Memory Pillow

Search your family collections or antique shops for richly decorated vintage linens—then stitch a treasure trove of memories into a keepsake pillow. See photo on page 26.

Project Specifications

Skill Level: Beginner
Pillow Size: Any Size

Materials

- Vintage linens of choice
- Scraps of cotton fabric for yo-yos
- Buttons and charms of choice
- Ribbon for bow
- Doily of choice
- Silk embroidery ribbon to match fabrics
- Green pearl cotton
- All-purpose thread to match fabrics
- Pillow form
- Water-soluble marker
- Basic sewing supplies and tools

Instructions

Note: Each memory pillow will be different, depending on the linens and memories you use. Choose colors to match some of the old fabrics and build your supplies from that.

Pillow

Step 1. Decide what part of the vintage linen you want to use as a pillow front, then measure for the top of the pillow, keeping in mind the size of your pillow form. Add 1" to pillow form size and cut out linen for front and back.

Step 2. To make yo-yos, cut desired number and sizes of fabric circles using patterns. With wrong side of fabric facing you, fold over on dotted line and stitch near edge around the outside of circle. Pull thread tight to form a

closed circle, tucking in raw edges. Tie off tightly.

Step 3. Place doily on pillow top and stitch in place. Sew yo-yos, buttons and trinkets in place.

Step 4. If there are plain areas to fill, draw ivy and baby's breath design with water-soluble marker. Stitch vine with green pearl cotton. Make French knots with silk embroidery ribbon as shown in Fig. 1.

Step 5. With right sides of pillow together, stitch around three sides using ½" seam allowance. Clip corners and turn. Insert pillow form and slipstitch the opening closed.

—By Karen Mead

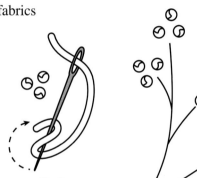

Medium Yo-yo

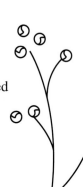

Fig. 1
Make French Knot as shown.

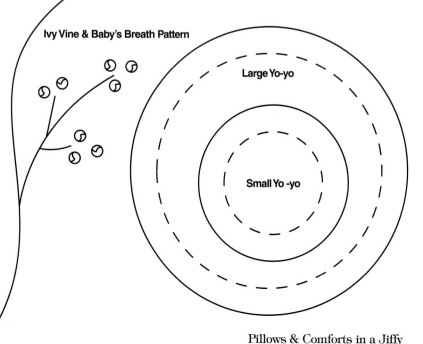

Ivy Vine & Baby's Breath Pattern

Large Yo-yo

Small Yo-yo

Floral Pillow

Thread-painting decorator fabric, leftover from a home design project or a sample of something you love, adds dimension and character to a decorator pillow. See photo on page 26.

Project Specifications

Skill Level: Beginner

Pillow Size: Any size

Materials

- Floral decorator fabric yardage as needed
- Tear-away stabilizer
- Coordinating ruffle fabric yardage as needed
- Square pillow insert
- All-purpose thread to match fabric
- Machine-embroidery thread a shade lighter than fabric details
- Basic sewing supplies and tools

Instructions

Yardage and Cutting

Step 1. For pillow front, measure a square the same size as pillow insert with floral motif centered. Add 1" seam allowance. For pillow back, use same dimensions as top, adding 6" to one side of square. Cut piece in half.

Step 2. For length of ruffle strip, multiply the length of one side of pillow by 4. Multiply that length by 3½. Width of strip is 5" for a pillow 18" square or larger; 4" for smaller pillows.

Construction

Step 1. Sew a ¼" hem on one long side of each backing piece.

Step 2. Sew short ends of ruffle strips together. Hem one long edge.

Step 3. With fabric stabilizer under pillow top, "thread-paint" selected details of floral print with machine satin-stitch to embellish. Do not outline around an entire area or it will appear to be appliqué. Select lines to accentuate such as flower centers, large leaves, petals, etc. Let thread colors overlap.

Step 4. Gather ruffle. Baste and sew to pillow front as shown in Fig. 1. Allow extra gathers at corners so ruffle will be full and generous.

Step 5. Baste front, right side up with ruffle facing

inward, to backing pieces, overlapped and facing down as shown in Fig. 2.

Step 6. Sew together. Trim seam allowance, clip curves at corners. Turn right side out and insert pillow.

—By Judi Kaufman

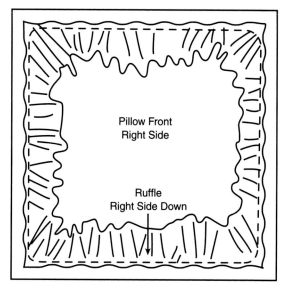

Fig. 1
Baste gathered ruffle to pillow top as shown.

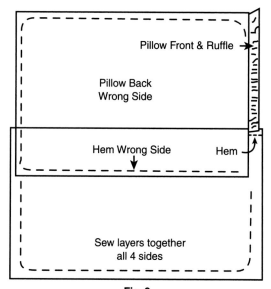

Fig. 2
Sew pillow pieces together with pillow front and back pieces right sides together as shown.

Wheelchair Throw

Spread some warmth and cheer at your local nursing home by stitching a few bright throws!
Big pockets are a practical solution for stashing tissues, eyeglasses and other necessities.

Project Specifications

Skill Level: Beginner
Wheelchair Throw Size: Approximately 36" x 42"

Materials

- 1 yard primary-colored print fleece
- 12" x 34" green fleece
- 9" x 16" yellow fleece
- 5 yards red braid trim
- All-purpose thread to match fabrics
- Basic sewing supplies and tools

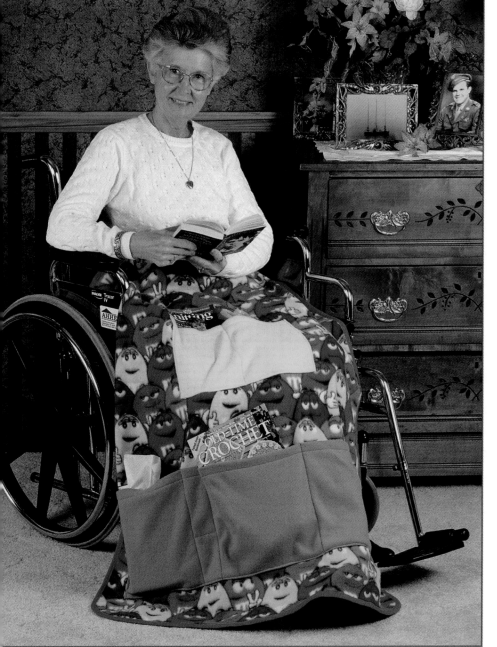

Instructions

Step 1. Round corners of primary-colored fleece and stitch red braid trim around outside edges.

Step 2. Stitch a 1" hem along one long side of green and yellow fleece. Press under ½" along other long side and ends.

Step 3. Center green pocket strip 4" from bottom of throw and stitch in place. Mark and stitch divider sections as shown in Fig. 1.

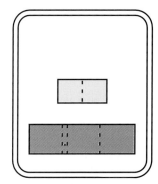

Fig. 1
Stitch green and yellow pockets to throw. Stitch dividers as shown.

Step 4. Center yellow pocket strip above green strip as shown in Fig. 1 and stitch in place. Mark and stitch divider sections.

—*By Sandy Garrett*

Stadium Throw & Tote

Choose the team colors of your favorite dedicated sports fan to make this cozy stadium set. The lucky, warm spectator will be proud to show his or her colors!

Project Specifications

Skill Level: Beginner
Throw Size: 58" x 76"
Tote Size: 18" x 18" x 2"

Materials

- 1½ yards royal blue fleece
- 1½ yards yellow fleece
- All-purpose thread to match fabrics
- Basic sewing supplies and tools

Instructions

Stadium Throw

Note: Use ½" seam allowance throughout.

Step 1. From each fabric cut four 20" x 30" rectangles.

Step 2. With right sides together stitch blue and yellow rectangles together in two strips as shown in Fig. 1. Press seams open and topstitch along each side of seam.

Step 3. Stitch two strips together as shown in Fig. 2. Press seam open and topstitch along each side of seam.

Step 4. Stitch a ½" hem around the outside edge; press.

Tote

Step 1. From each fabric cut four squares 10" x 10", one strip 3" x 55" from royal blue and one strip 3" x 40" from yellow.

Step 2. Stitch front and back tote squares together in same manner as for throw, referring to Fig. 3 for placement. Press seams and topstitch.

Step 3. Fold over and stitch a ½" hem along one edge of each section.

Step 4. Beginning with raw edge of strip ½" above hemmed edge with right sides together, stitch royal blue 3" strip along one side of one block. Continue around corners of block until reaching hemmed edge of other side. Strip should extend ½" above edge. Repeat with second block and other side of 3" royal blue strip.

Step 5. Stitch the yellow strip to the tops of the royal blue strip, right sides together. Fold in edges of yellow strip the

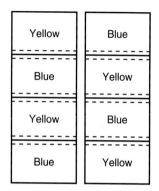

Fig. 1
Stitch rectangles together as shown to form strips.

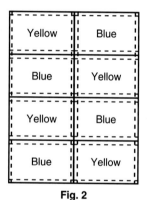

Fig. 2
Stitch two strips together as shown.

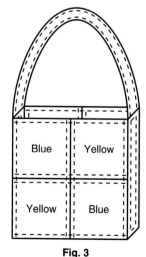

Fig. 3
Stitch front and back tote squares together as shown.

same width as blue strips and topstitch along raw edges.

Step 6. Fold throw and insert in bag.

—By Sandy Garrett

Rooster Pillow

*You'll have something to crow about when you complete
this proud rooster—colorful and ready for a barnyard frolic.*

Project Specifications

Skill Level: Beginner
Pillow Size: 14" x 14"

Materials

- 15" x 15" square chicken-wire fabric for pillow top
- 15" x 15" square black cotton fabric for pillow back
- Scraps of slate blue, purple, olive green, gold, dark red, cream, tan, beige, rust, brown, navy and dark green felt
- 14" pillow form
- 6-strand embroidery floss to match each felt color
- 1 black shank button for eye
- All-purpose thread to match fabrics
- Water-soluble marker
- Basic sewing supplies and tools

Instructions

Step 1. Trace and cut all rooster fabrics as directed on patterns.

Step 2. Referring to Fig. 1, lay out rooster pieces on blank sheet of paper in order, starting with piece 1.

Step 3. Center paper and rooster pieces on chicken-wire square and carefully slide paper out from under rooster.

Step 4. Starting with piece 18, remove one piece at a time after tracing around its shape with water-soluble marker.

Step 5. Place piece 1, layering over feet (pieces 12 and 13). Buttonhole-stitch in place with 1 strand of matching embroidery floss.

Step 6. Continue adding, in order, pieces 3–11, buttonhole-stitching each with 1 strand of matching embroidery floss and leaving open top sides of pieces 4 and 5.

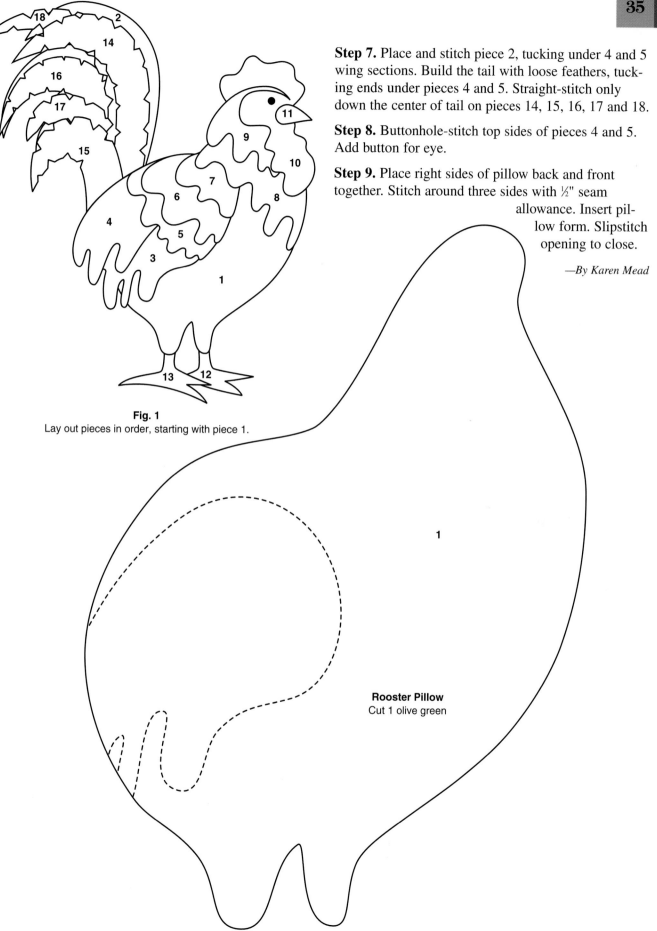

Fig. 1
Lay out pieces in order, starting with piece 1.

Step 7. Place and stitch piece 2, tucking under 4 and 5 wing sections. Build the tail with loose feathers, tucking ends under pieces 4 and 5. Straight-stitch only down the center of tail on pieces 14, 15, 16, 17 and 18.

Step 8. Buttonhole-stitch top sides of pieces 4 and 5. Add button for eye.

Step 9. Place right sides of pillow back and front together. Stitch around three sides with ½" seam allowance. Insert pillow form. Slipstitch opening to close.

—*By Karen Mead*

Rooster Pillow
Cut 1 olive green

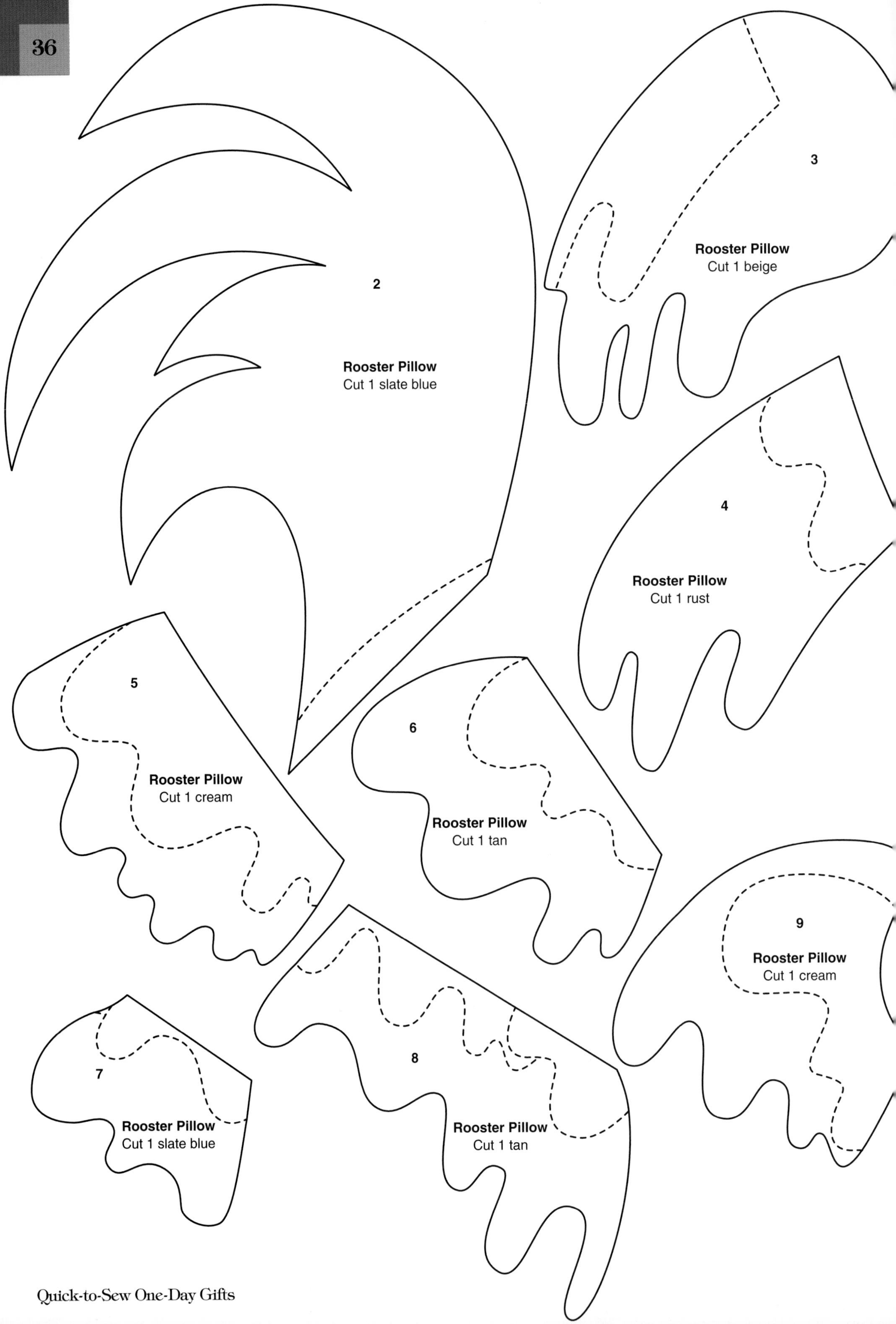

2

Rooster Pillow
Cut 1 slate blue

3

Rooster Pillow
Cut 1 beige

4

Rooster Pillow
Cut 1 rust

5

Rooster Pillow
Cut 1 cream

6

Rooster Pillow
Cut 1 tan

9

Rooster Pillow
Cut 1 cream

7

Rooster Pillow
Cut 1 slate blue

8

Rooster Pillow
Cut 1 tan

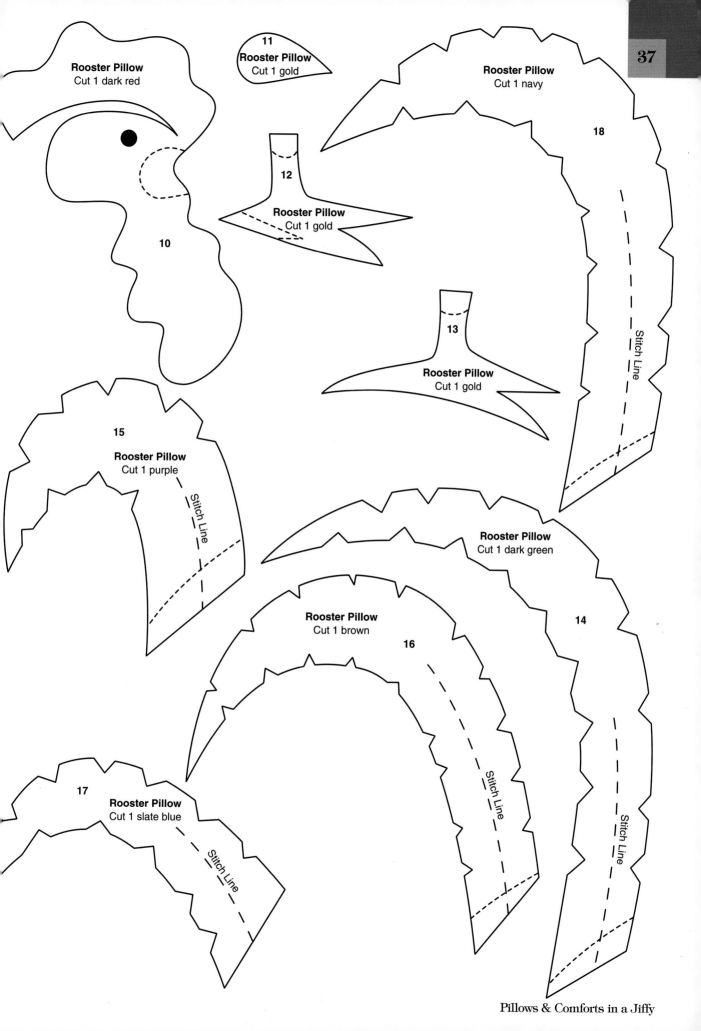

Rooster Pillow
Cut 1 dark red

10

11
Rooster Pillow
Cut 1 gold

12
Rooster Pillow
Cut 1 gold

13
Rooster Pillow
Cut 1 gold

Rooster Pillow
Cut 1 navy

18

Stitch Line

15
Rooster Pillow
Cut 1 purple

Stitch Line

Rooster Pillow
Cut 1 dark green

14

Rooster Pillow
Cut 1 brown

16

Stitch Line

Stitch Line

17
Rooster Pillow
Cut 1 slate blue

Stitch Line

Holiday Pillow Covers

Silver and gold, glimmer and shine—all festive holiday looks to dress up your own everyday pillows for holiday entertaining or to give to your special friends.

Project Specifications

Skill Level: Beginner
Envelope Cover Size: Any Size
Neck Roll Cover Size: Approximately 16" x 6"
Round Cover Size: Any Size

Materials

For Envelope Pillow
- 1¼ yards silver lamé piping
- Square pillow

For Neck Roll Pillow
- 2 yards silver ribbon
- Neck roll pillow 6" x 16"

For Round Pillow
- 1¾ yards gold lamé piping
- Round pillow

For each pillow
- ⅝ yard glitter organza fabric
- All-purpose thread to blend with fabrics
- Basic sewing supplies and tools

Instructions

Envelope Pillow

Step 1. To determine fabric-cutting size, measure around pillow as shown in Fig. 1. Divide that number by 2 and add 1" for two ½" seam allowances. (If pillow measures 28" around: 14" + 1" = 15".)

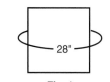
Fig. 1
Measure around pillow as shown.

Step 2. For length, measure around pillow, multiply by 3 and add 1" for seam allowances. (If pillow measures 28" around: 14" x 3" + 1" = 43".)

Step 3. Cut fabric rectangle based on dimensions determined above. Press hem at one short end to wrong side

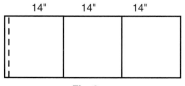
Fig. 2
Mark hemmed fabric in 3 equal parts.

and stitch in place. Mark remaining length in three equal parts as shown in Fig. 2.

Step 4. Fold fabric in half lengthwise. From folded side, draw a diagonal line from the end to ½" above point A. Cut along this line forming a point as shown in Fig. 3.

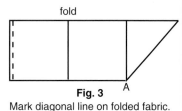
Fig. 3
Mark diagonal line on folded fabric.

Step 5. Sew piping to right side along pointed end of rectangle. Turn raw edge of piping to the under side and topstitch in place.

Step 6. With right sides together, fold the hemmed edge to the flap edge as shown in Fig. 4 and stitch both sides with a ½" seam allowance.

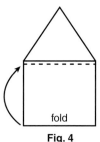
Fig. 4
Fold hemmed edge to flap edge as shown.

Step 7. Turn right side out, press and slip pillow in the envelope.

Neck Roll Pillow

Step 1. Cut a fabric rectangle 19" x 31". Sew a narrow hem on each short end.

Step 2. With right sides together, fold in half lengthwise and stitch long edge with a ½" seam allowance, leaving both ends open.

Step 3. Slide pillow into sleeve and center. Gather each end and tie with ribbon or streamers.

Round Pillow

Step 1. Measure diameter of pillow (14" for this example) and add 4" for a 1½" flange and ½" seam allowance. Cut a square (14" + 4" = 18") of fabric this measurement.

Step 2. Fold square in half twice. Starting at corner of folds, measure one half of above measurement out

Continued on page 43

Lamb Hot-Water Bottle Cover

Nothing feels better on a cold winter night than toasty-warm toes, so trust this cuddly little lame to add some fun to the functional hot-water bottle.

Project Specifications

Skill Level: Beginner
Water Bottle Cover Size: 14" x 7½"

Materials

- White chenille 17" x 28"
- ⅓ yard white flannel
- ¼ yard black satin fabric
- 18" (1"-wide) pink ribbon
- White 6-strand embroidery floss
- Polyester fiberfill
- Hot-water bottle
- Black and white all-purpose thread
- Embroidery needle
- Basic sewing supplies and tools

Instructions

Note: Use ⅜" seam allowance throughout.

Step 1. Trace and cut feet, tail, ears, head and face as directed on patterns.

Step 2. Cut a 15" x 9½" rectangle of paper for lamb body pattern. Use a dinner plate to round the pattern corners as shown in Fig. 1. Use pattern to cut one body front from chenille and one from flannel.

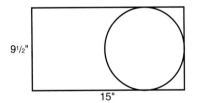

9½"

15"

Fig. 1
Use dinner plate to round corners of pattern.

Step 3. Cut body front pattern in half. Extend cut edge of one half by ½" and the other half by 2½" as shown in Fig. 2. Use patterns to cut body back pieces from chenille and flannel.

Step 4. Trace eyelid line on one face. Use 2 strands of white embroidery floss to embroider eyelid lines.

Step 5. With right sides together, sew front and back pieces of ears, face, tail, feet and head. Leave tops

open for stuffing. Clip curves and turn; press. Topstitch lines marked on feet.

Step 6. Very lightly stuff tail, feet, face and head with polyester fiberfill. Use eraser end of pencil to work fiberfill down against all seams. Pin openings on tail and feet closed. Slipstitch the openings on face and head closed.

Step 7. With right sides together, stitch flannel and chenille back body pieces together along center line. Press seams open. Fold flannel back to line the chenille; topstitch along the center lines as shown in Fig. 3.

Step 8. Zigzag remaining edges of chenille and flannel body back parts together. With wrong sides together, zigzag body front parts together.

Step 9. Pin feet 3" apart on one long side of body front and tail at top of curve as shown in Fig. 4.

Step 10. Chenille sides together, place body back pieces over top with finished

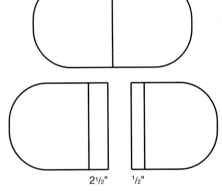

2½"   ½"

Fig. 2
Extend cut edges of body back as shown.

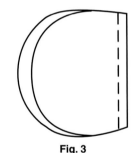

Fig. 3
Topstitch along center lines of body back pieces.

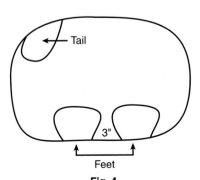

Tail

3"

Feet

Fig. 4
Place feet and tail on body front as shown.

edges overlapping in the center. Pin and stitch around the periphery. Turn right side out through back opening.

Step 11. Slightly gather top edges of ears and pin to sides of face. Zigzag-stitch across top edge of face, catching the top of ears at the sides.

Step 12. Pin head across top of face and ears, covering all raw edges. Slipstitch the side and bottom edges of head to face and ears.

Step 13. Pin head unit to front at an angle as shown in photo. Slipstitch top of head and face to chenille.

Step 14. Tie a ribbon bow and stitch just below face.

—*By Barbara Matthiessen*

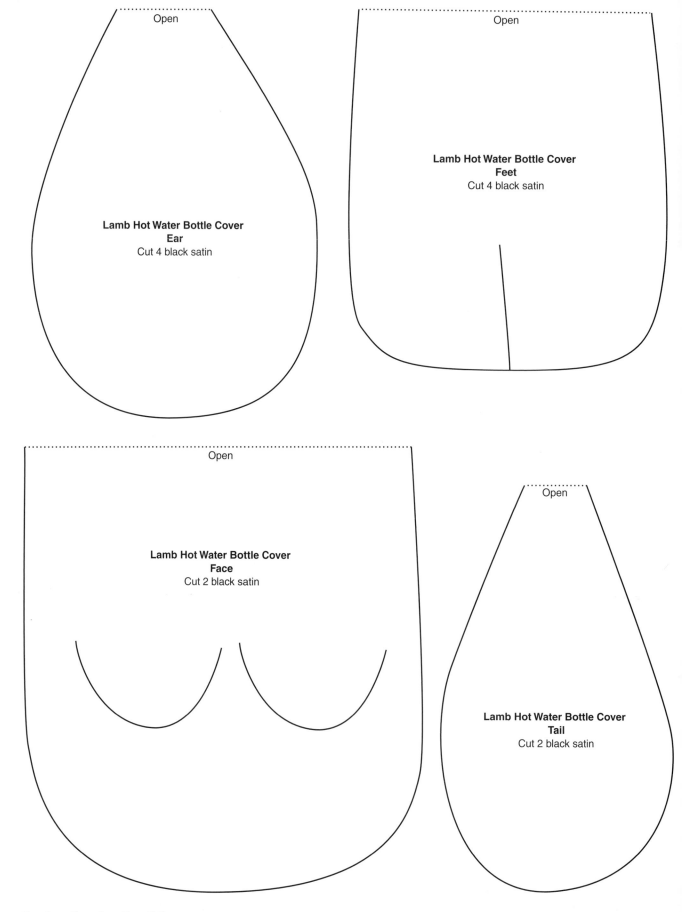

Open

Lamb Hot Water Bottle Cover
Ear
Cut 4 black satin

Open

Lamb Hot Water Bottle Cover
Feet
Cut 4 black satin

Open

Lamb Hot Water Bottle Cover
Face
Cut 2 black satin

Open

Lamb Hot Water Bottle Cover
Tail
Cut 2 black satin

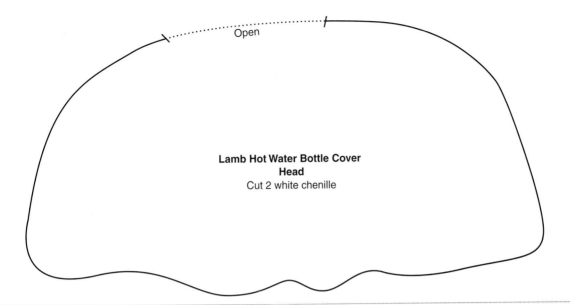

**Lamb Hot Water Bottle Cover
Head
Cut 2 white chenille**

Open

Holiday Pillow Covers

Continued from page 39

from corner and mark. Use this mark to draw a curve as shown in Fig. 5.

Step 3. From remaining fabric cut two rectangles half of the width of the square plus 1", and as wide as the square (10" x 18") as shown in Fig. 6.

Step 4. Wrong sides together, fold over and stitch a 1" hem along one long edge of each piece.

Step 5. With both right sides up, place one hem on top of the other as shown in Fig. 7 and baste in place.

Step 6. Using the first circle as a pattern, cut a circle from the hemmed piece as shown in Fig. 8.

Step 7. Stitch piping around outside edge of unhemmed circle.

Step 8. With right sides together, stitch the two circles together. Remove basting and turn right side out.

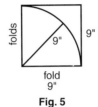

Fig. 5
Mark curve as shown to make circle.

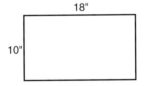

Fig. 6
Cut two rectangles as shown.

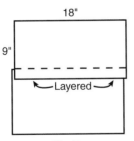

Fig. 7
Place one hem on top of the other as shown and baste.

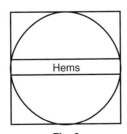

Fig. 8
Cut a circle from the hemmed piece as shown.

Step 9. Mark 1½" from outside edge and stitch, forming a flange as shown in Fig. 9. Insert pillow through hemmed opening in back.

—*By Sandy Gerret*

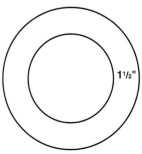

Fig. 9
Stitch 1½" from outside edge to form flange.

Quick-Time Kitchen Goodies

Come into my kitchen! Friends and loved ones seem to enjoy congregating in the kitchen. It's a comfortable place, full of the memories of fragrant treats and good times together. What better way to create a new memory than with a gift for the kitchen?

From nostalgic redwork to quick machine appliqué, this chapter is packed with projects to make memories!

Angel Apron and Oven Mitts

Every kitchen needs a guardian angel! This smiling little cherub will lift the cook's spirits and the oven mitts will be star attractions.

Project Specifications

Skill Level: Intermediate
Apron Size: All Sizes
Mitt Size: All Sizes

Materials

- ¼ yard white-on-white
- ¼ yard rose print
- 2 yards floral print
- ¼ yard coordinating print for mitt lining
- Scraps of pale pink, lavender, light brown, yellow plaid and yellow print for appliqué
- ¼ yard fusible transfer web
- 2¼ yards thin cotton batting
- Pink and brown 6-strand embroidery floss
- All-purpose threads to match fabrics
- Rayon thread to match appliqué pieces
- Gold metallic thread
- One package white corded piping
- Two packages wide bias tape for mitt piping
- 2 (¼") white buttons
- Rotary-cutting tools
- Basic sewing supplies and tools

Note: For safety, be sure to use cotton batting for oven mitts. Polyester may melt at high temperatures.

Instructions

Note: Use ¼" seam allowance throughout.

Apron

Step 1. Trace and cut apron bib and lining as directed on pattern.

Step 2. From rose print cut one strip 2" x 10" and one strip 2" x 14". Stitch across top and bottom of bib as shown in Fig. 1. Press and

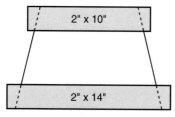

Fig. 1
Stitch strips across top and bottom of apron bib.

trim. Cut two strips 2" x 15" and stitch to each side of bib as shown in Fig. 2. Press and trim.

Step 3. From floral print cut one strip 2" x 18". Stitch across top of bordered bib. Cut two strips 2" x 22" and stitch to sides of bib as shown in Fig. 3. Press and trim.

Step 4. Cut cotton batting 14" x 20". Center wrong side of bib on batting. Topstitch around outside of bib using ⅛" seam allowance. Trim excess batting.

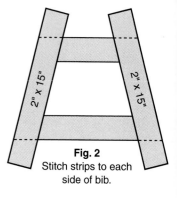

Fig. 2
Stitch strips to each side of bib.

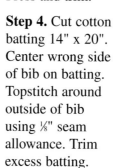

Fig. 3
Stitch strips to top and sides of bib.

Step 5. From floral print cut two 3" x 45" strips for ties. Fold each in half lengthwise with right sides facing. Stitch down long side and across end. Trim corners, turn right side out and press.

Step 6. Allowing for ¼" seam allowance at outside of apron bib, place folded edge of each tie toward the center of the apron bib as shown in Fig. 4. Stitch open end of each tie to top of bib with ⅛" seam allowance.

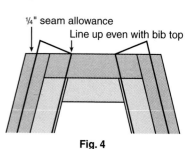

Fig. 4
Place ties on bib as shown

Step 7. Place right sides of bib and lining together. Stitch around three sides, leaving bottom open (be careful not to catch ties in seams). Trim, turn and press.

With white thread topstitch around white apron center. Topstitch open end closed with ⅛" seam allowance.

Step 8. From floral print cut two 1¾" x 22" strips for waistband. Center one strip across bottom edge of bib front and stitch. Center other strip across bottom edge of bib back and stitch.

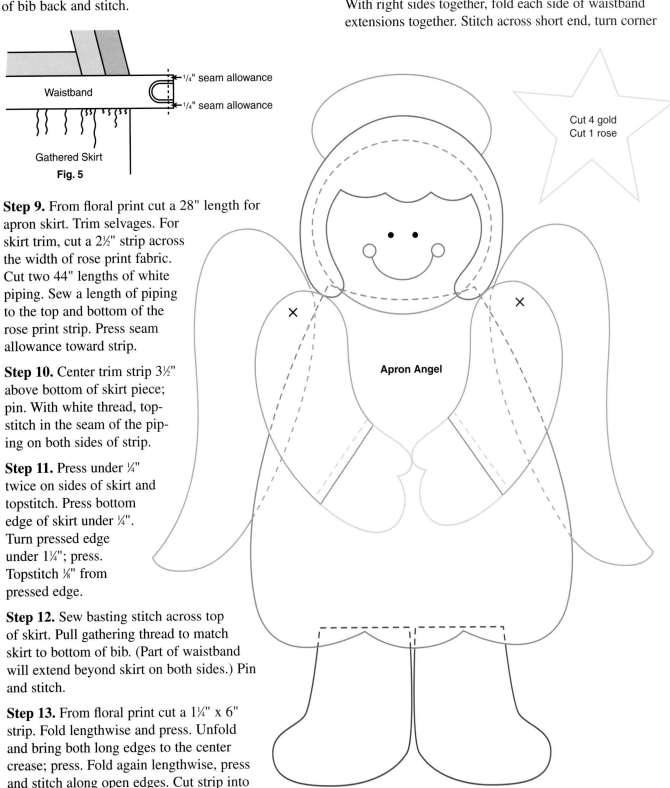

Waistband

¼" seam allowance
¼" seam allowance

Gathered Skirt

Fig. 5

Step 9. From floral print cut a 28" length for apron skirt. Trim selvages. For skirt trim, cut a 2½" strip across the width of rose print fabric. Cut two 44" lengths of white piping. Sew a length of piping to the top and bottom of the rose print strip. Press seam allowance toward strip.

Step 10. Center trim strip 3½" above bottom of skirt piece; pin. With white thread, topstitch in the seam of the piping on both sides of strip.

Step 11. Press under ¼" twice on sides of skirt and topstitch. Press bottom edge of skirt under ¼". Turn pressed edge under 1¼"; press. Topstitch ⅛" from pressed edge.

Step 12. Sew basting stitch across top of skirt. Pull gathering thread to match skirt to bottom of bib. (Part of waistband will extend beyond skirt on both sides.) Pin and stitch.

Step 13. From floral print cut a 1¼" x 6" strip. Fold lengthwise and press. Unfold and bring both long edges to the center crease; press. Fold again lengthwise, press and stitch along open edges. Cut strip into

two 3" pieces. Make a loop with each piece and pin raw ends to each end of front waistband, allowing ¼" seam allowance on each side of loop as shown in Fig. 5. Topstitch using ⅛" seam allowance.

Step 14. Press raw edge of back waistband under ¼". With right sides together, fold each side of waistband extensions together. Stitch across short end, turn corner

Cut 4 gold
Cut 1 rose

Apron Angel

and stitch 3" more. Trim corners and turn waistband extensions right side out; press. Pin and then stitch back waistband to skirt by hand.

Appliqué

Step 1. Trace appliqué shapes onto paper side of fusible transfer web; cut out leaving roughly ½" margin around shapes.

Step 2. Fuse to wrong side of selected fabrics according to manufacturer's directions and cut out on tracing line.

Step 3. Position appliqué pieces, referring to photo; fuse in place.

Step 4. With matching rayon thread, satin-stitch around pieces.

Step 5. With pencil draw halo and satin-stitch with gold metallic thread.

Step 6. Buttonhole-stitch with gold metallic thread around rose print star.

Step 7. To complete angel's face, use 4 strands of brown embroidery floss to sew a French knot for each eye. Use pink floss to backstitch the mouth and satin-stitch the cheeks.

Step 8. Sew a button to each shoulder.

Oven Mitts

Note: Makes one left and one right.

Step 1. Trace and cut oven mitts as directed on pattern.

Step 2. Trace stars onto paper side of fusible transfer web. Cut four additional stars ¼" larger than small star pattern and two stars ¼" larger than large star pattern.

Step 3. Fuse to wrong side of fabrics according to manufacturer's directions. Additional stars should all be fused to yellow plaid. Cut out on tracing lines.

Step 4. Position appliqué pieces, referring to photo. Place a yellow plaid star of appropriate size under each star appliqué. Fuse in layers. Satin-stitch around each inner star with matching colors. Buttonhole-stitch around each yellow plaid star.

Step 5. Make four stacks of oven mitt batting shapes. Place one stack of four on wrong side of each lining piece. Place wrong side of floral print on top of each stack. Topstitch around each stack with ⅛" seam allowance.

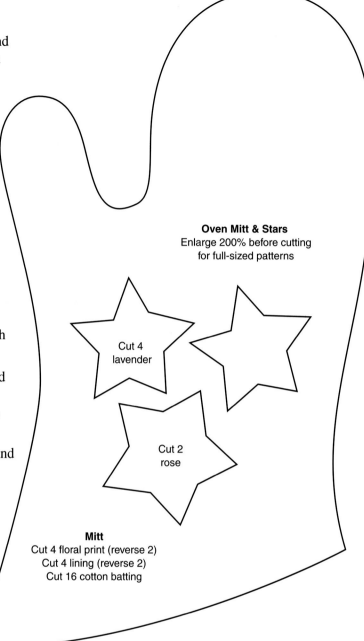

Oven Mitt & Stars
Enlarge 200% before cutting
for full-sized patterns

Cut 4
lavender

Cut 2
rose

Mitt
Cut 4 floral print (reverse 2)
Cut 4 lining (reverse 2)
Cut 16 cotton batting

Step 6. Cut four 8½" lengths of bias tape. Stitch one piece along top floral print lower edge of each mitt section. Fold the bias tape over the seam allowance to the lining side and hand-stitch in place.

Step 7. With lining sides together, pin right mitt sections together. Topstitch using ⅛" seam allowance. Repeat for left mitt.

Step 8. Allowing a 6" length for a hanging loop at the beginning, stitch bias tape around outside front of mitts. Turn under ½" at the end. Turn bias tape to back of mitts and hand-stitch in place. Make a loop with the 6" length and stitch together.

—By Michele Crawford

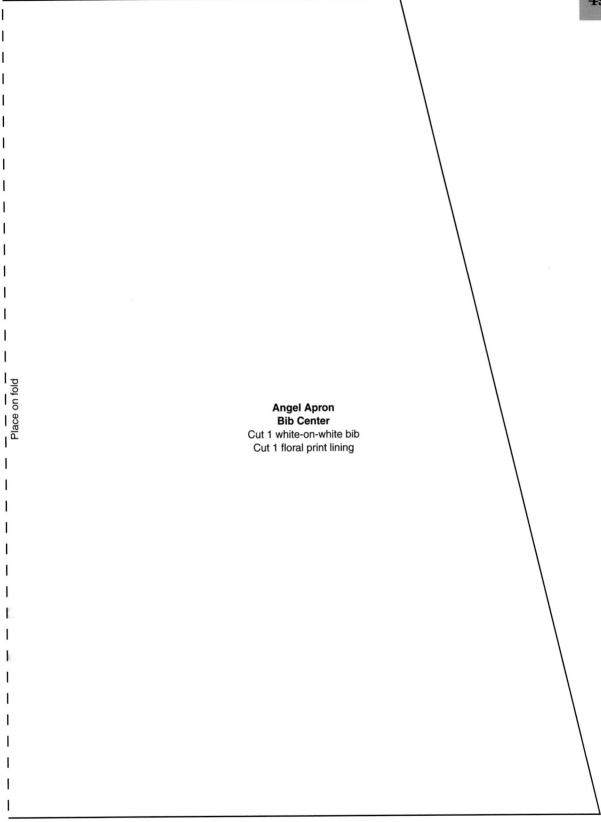

Place on fold

Angel Apron
Bib Center
Cut 1 white-on-white bib
Cut 1 floral print lining

Veggie Kitchen Set

This collection—colorful big and bold veggies with eye-catching appeal and crisp black-and-white checkerboard trim—will add some zing to the kitchen!

Project Specifications

Skill Level: Beginner
Table Runner Size: 38" x 17"
Place Mat Size: 20" x 17"
Pot Holder Size: 8½" x 10½"

Materials

For Each Place Mat
- Black fabric, medium weight, 19½" x 16½"
- ¼ yard yellow fabric
- ¼ yard black-and-white checkerboard fabric with 1⅛" squares
- ¼ yard fusible webbing

For Table Runner
- ½ yard medium-weight black fabric
- ½ yard red print fabric
- ¼ yard black-and-white checkerboard fabric with 1⅛" squares
- Low-loft cotton batting strips two each ¾" x 15" and ¾" x 38"
- ½ yard fusible webbing

For Pot Holders
- ¼ yard each green, red, yellow and purple 100 percent cotton fabrics
- ½ yard black-and-white checkerboard fabric with 1⅛" squares
- 15" length of black bias tape
- Old ironing board cover
- ¼ yard low-loft cotton batting

Note: For safety, be sure to use cotton fabric and batting for pot holders. Polyester may melt at high temperatures.

For all pieces in set
- Black all-purpose sewing thread
- Black decorative thread
- Vegetable stamps
- Green, red, orange, purple, yellow and white acrylic fabric paint
- Small artist paintbrushes (round and flat)
- Basic sewing supplies and tools

Instructions

Place Mat

Step 1. Cut one strip each 6½" x 18" yellow fabric and fusible transfer web.

Step 2. Cut two border strips from checkerboard fabric 3½" x 17" and one strip 3½" x 18", placing on fabric as shown in Fig. 1.

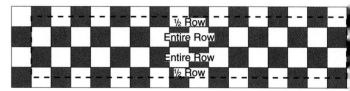

Fig. 1
Cut border strips as shown, including 2 full rows down the center and ½ row on each side.

Step 3. Fuse one side fusible webbing to wrong side of yellow fabric.

Step 4. Make a cardboard or plastic template for sawtooth pattern. Trace along one edge of yellow fabric backed with fusible web, repositioning template to span entire length. Cut along traced sawtooth pattern.

Step 5. Referring to photo, stamp vegetable images onto yellow fabric following paint manufacturer's directions. Augment, shade and highlight, if desired, by mixing colors and applying with small brushes to stamped designs. Allow to dry completely before sewing.

Step 6. Press border pieces in half lengthwise, wrong sides together; press. Turn under ½" on each long edge as shown in Fig. 2. Sew border pieces together by unfolding along center line, matching blocks and sewing as shown in Fig. 3, keeping turned-under edges turned under. Trim corners. Turn right side out and press. You now have a three-sided frame.

Fig. 2
Fold border strips in half lengthwise, wrong sides together; press.
Turn under ½" on each long edge.

Step 7. Place black fabric on flat surface and align

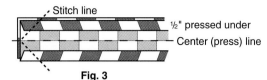

Fig. 3
Unfold strips along center line, match blocks
with right sides together and sew as shown,
keeping edges turned under.

frame around edges, tucking raw edges of black fabric into frame. Adjust if necessary to square. Sew through all layers along border inner edge using straight stitch and black all-purpose thread or black decorative button-hole stitch and decorative thread. (Border will not go all the way to end because yellow fabric will cover it.)

Step 8. Fuse yellow fabric to left side of mat, turning under ½" at left edge, bottom and top to fuse to back side of mat. Finish saw-tooth edge with decorative stitching.

Table Runner

Step 1. Cut black fabric 16½" x 37½".

Step 2. Cut two border strips each 3½" x 39" and 3½" x 18", as shown in Fig. 1.

Step 3. Cut red print fabric and fusible web as shown on Table Runner Contrast Material Pattern. Fuse web to wrong side of fabric.

Step 4. Make a cardboard or plastic template for saw-tooth pattern. Trace along edge of red fabric backed with fusible web, repositioning template to span entire length. Cut along traced sawtooth pattern.

Step 5. Fuse red fabric to black rectangle, aligning top and left edges. Finish sawtooth edge with decorative stitching (buttonhole or zigzag).

Step 6. Repeat Place Mat Step 6, but complete four-sided frame.

Step 7. Place runner on flat surface and tuck into frame. Adjust to square, if necessary (a gridded mat helps). Tuck strips of batting into frame so it is encased as shown in Fig. 4. Pin and sew through all

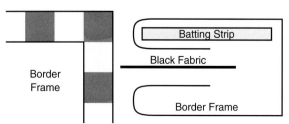

Fig. 4
Tuck batting into border frame as shown.

layers along border inner edge using straight stitch and black all-purpose thread or black decorative stitch and decorative thread. Press.

Step 8. Referring to photo, carefully stamp vegetable images onto runner after first practicing technique on scrap fabrics, following manufacturer's directions. Augment, shade and highlight, if desired, by mixing colors and applying with small brushes to stamped design. Dry completely.

Pot Holders

Step 1. Cut pot holder back pieces as directed on pattern.

Step 2. Cut border pieces as directed on pattern, lining up checks identically as shown in Fig. 5.

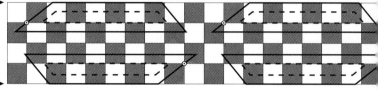

Fig. 5
To cut pot holder border strips, pick a reference point
and place each piece identically as shown.

Step 3. Stamp vegetables as in Table Runner Step 8.

Step 4. Each pot holder has two border pieces and two reversed border pieces placed alternately around its edge. Match checks carefully and sew ends with ½" seams. Press seams open.

Step 5. Cut pot holder front from matching color using solid red of Pot Holder Back as outside edge. Cut pot holder backing piece from matching color using Pot Holder Back pattern and trimming shorter end off along cutting line.

Step 6. Align a stamped front piece on center of batting piece and using black all-purpose thread or decorative thread stitch around vegetable design to outline and pad. Loosely pull each corner of top fabric to center and pin temporarily to hold out of the way.

Step 7. Fold one backing piece along fold line and press. Trim ¾" from fold. Turn raw edge under again and hem. Repeat for each color.

Step 8. Stack pieces as follows for one pot holder: front piece, batting side up, corners still pinned to the center; ironing board cover; whole back, right side up; hemmed back, right side up (point goes at top of veggie design); ending with completed border wrong side up. Align edges and pin in place. Sew ½" seam. Trim corners and at top and bottom points trim along

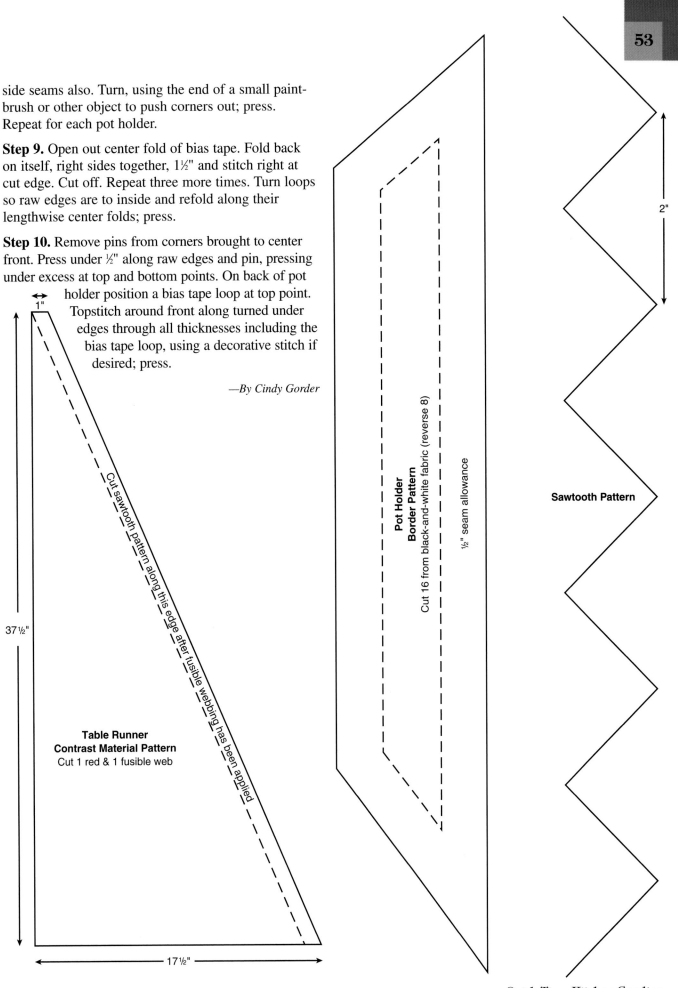

side seams also. Turn, using the end of a small paint-brush or other object to push corners out; press. Repeat for each pot holder.

Step 9. Open out center fold of bias tape. Fold back on itself, right sides together, 1½" and stitch right at cut edge. Cut off. Repeat three more times. Turn loops so raw edges are to inside and refold along their lengthwise center folds; press.

Step 10. Remove pins from corners brought to center front. Press under ½" along raw edges and pin, pressing under excess at top and bottom points. On back of pot holder position a bias tape loop at top point. Topstitch around front along turned under edges through all thicknesses including the bias tape loop, using a decorative stitch if desired; press.

—By Cindy Gorder

1"

37½"

Cut sawtooth pattern along this edge after fusible webbing has been applied

**Table Runner
Contrast Material Pattern**
Cut 1 red & 1 fusible web

17½"

**Pot Holder
Border Pattern**
Cut 16 from black-and-white fabric (reverse 8)

½" seam allowance

2"

Sawtooth Pattern

53

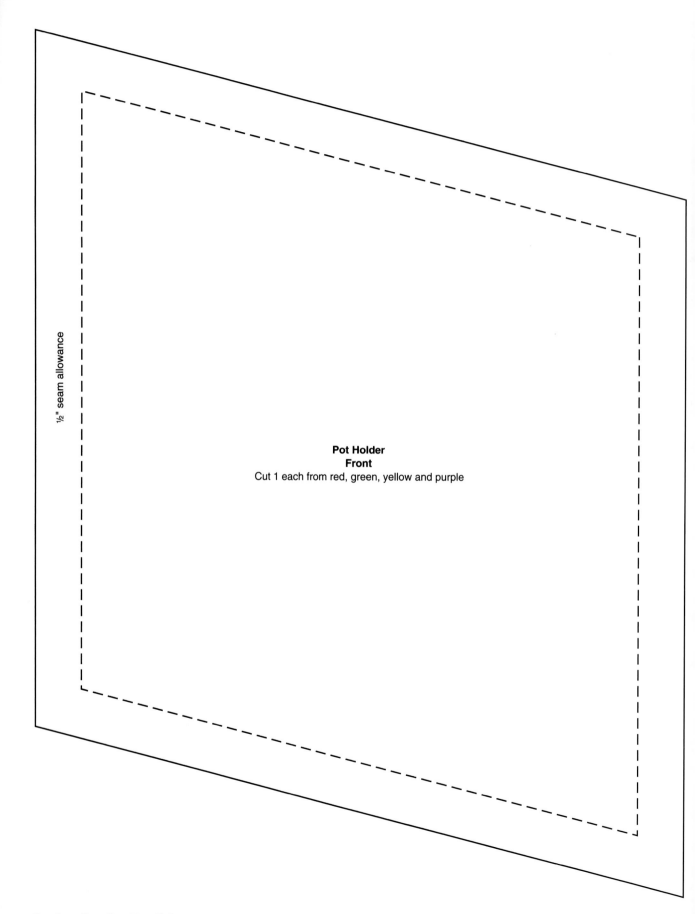

½" seam allowance

Pot Holder
Front
Cut 1 each from red, green, yellow and purple

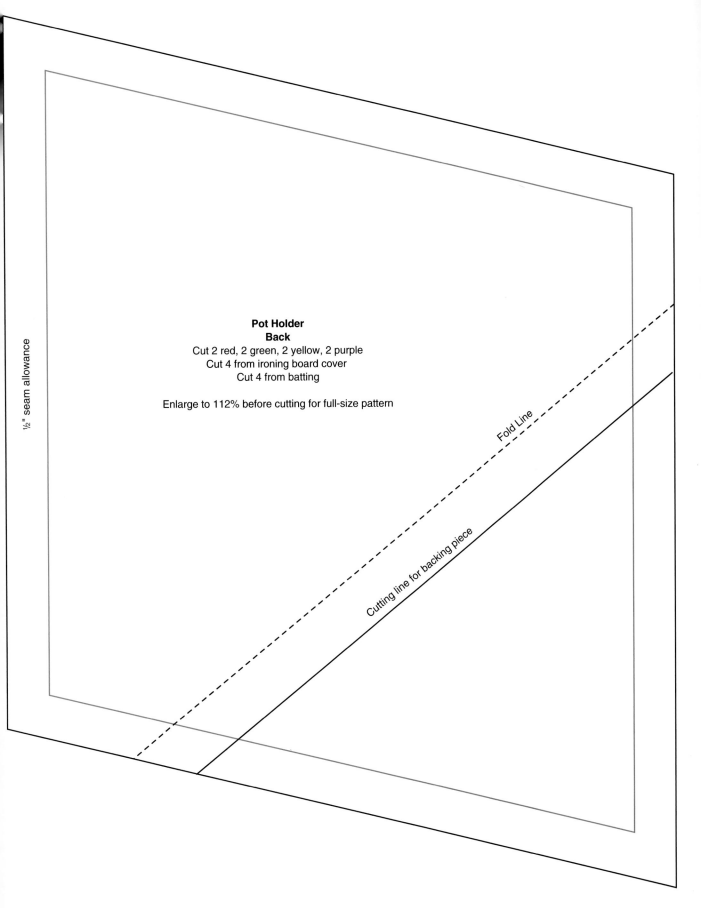

½" seam allowance

Pot Holder
Back
Cut 2 red, 2 green, 2 yellow, 2 purple
Cut 4 from ironing board cover
Cut 4 from batting

Enlarge to 112% before cutting for full-size pattern

Fold Line

Cutting line for backing piece

Teapot Wall Quilt

First worked as "penny squares" in the 1930s, redwork is enjoying a comeback.
And no wonder! Everyone loves traditional red and white patterns.

Project Specifications

Skill Level: Beginner

Wall Quilt Size: 13" x 15"

Materials

- ¼ yard red-and-cream print fabric
- ½ yard muslin
- Thin batting 15" x 17"
- ⅔ yard (⅜"-wide) cream ribbon
- 4 (¾") cream buttons
- 1 skein red 6-strand embroidery floss
- Natural all-purpose thread
- Water-soluble marker
- Basic sewing supplies and tools

Instructions

Step 1. Cut two pieces of muslin 10½" x 12½". Fold one piece in each direction to find center. Mark a center dot with water-soluble marker.

Step 2. Use water-soluble marker to trace teapot design onto muslin, matching center dot of pattern with center dot of muslin.

Step 3. Baste the two pieces of muslin together and stitch the teapot design using straight stitch and 2 strands of red embroidery floss.

Center

Teapot Wall Quilt
Enlarge to 125% for full-size pattern

Step 4. Stitch flower and vine design using straight stitch and 1 strand of red embroidery floss. Work lazy-daisy stitches for leaves. Add French knots in center of flowers with 2 strands of red floss.

Step 5. From red-and-cream print fabric cut two strips each 2" x 12½" and 2" x 13½". Stitch shorter strips to top and bottom of muslin; press. Stitch longer strips to sides of piece; press.

Step 6. Cut muslin backing piece 15" x 17". With design facing the backing muslin, place both on batting piece. Trim all layers to match top.

Step 7. Stitch around periphery with ¼" seam allowance. Leave 4" opening in one side for turning. Turn, press and slipstitch opening closed.

Step 8. Sew buttons in corners referring to photo. Cut ribbon in two pieces and stitch at midpoint near each top border seam again referring to photo.

—By Karen Mead

Welcome Rug and Wall Banner

Working with felt is quick and easy—colors are great and finishing is minimal.
This set would be a breeze to make and present as a special housewarming gift.

Project Specifications

Skill Level: Beginner
Rug Size: 32" x 16"
Wall Banner Size: 9" x 12"

Materials

- 36" x 36" burgundy felt
- 36" x 36" dark green felt
- 18" x 24" gold felt
- ¼ yard plaid fabric to coordinate with felt
- 1 spool all-purpose burgundy thread
- 1 skein gold pearl cotton
- 2 (⅜") gold shank buttons for doorknobs
- 6 (⅝") black shank buttons
- 6 (½") brown buttons
- 12 assorted buttons for wire
- 12" square white cardboard
- 1 yard #18 craft wire for hanger
- 5" x 7" potpourri packet
- Glue gun (optional)
- Basic sewing supplies and tools

Instructions

Welcome Rug

Step 1. Cut a paper rectangle 16" x 32". Round one long side for a half-circle shape as shown in Fig. 1. Using this pattern, cut two burgundy felt pieces. Cut a dark green felt piece 1" smaller all around.

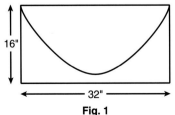

Fig. 1
Round one side of rectangle as shown.

Step 2. From gold felt cut a house as directed on house pattern. Cut WELCOME letters from burgundy felt. Cut two 2" x 2" gold felt squares.

Step 3. Referring to photo, sew house in center of dark green piece using machine- or hand-buttonhole

stitch and burgundy thread. Cut four fabric squares 2" x 2" and one piece 2" x 4". Sew larger piece to house for door. Sew 2 squares to house as shown in photo, slightly overlapping corners in center.

Step 4. Overlap two gold felt squares with two fabric squares and place on each side of house.

Step 5. Machine- or hand-stitch letters in place.

Step 6. Center green felt piece on one burgundy piece. With burgundy thread, buttonhole-stitch around periphery of green felt.

Step 7. Place two burgundy pieces one on top of the other and, with gold pearl cotton, buttonhole-stitch around periphery.

Step 8. Tear ½" strips of plaid fabric and tie three 3" bows with 4" tails. Stitch bows to rug as shown in photo. Stitch a black shank button in center of each bow and one on each pair of patches. With pearl cotton, tie two brown buttons on each set of patches. Sew gold button to door for doorknob.

Wall Banner

Step 1. Cut house pieces as directed on pattern. Cut one 6" x 6" square dark green felt.

Step 2. From burgundy felt cut HOME letters. From fabric cut two 2" x 2" squares and one piece 2" x 4".

Step 3. Referring to photo throughout, machine- or hand-stitch letters, squares and door in place.

Step 4. Make three bows as in Rug Step 8. Referring to photo, sew one bow to house. Sew one black shank button and two brown buttons to bow. Sew gold button to door.

Step 5. Stitch 6" x 6" green felt square to back of green house to make a pocket as shown in Fig. 2.

Step 6. Cut piece of white cardboard ¼" smaller all around than gold house. Place it between the gold and green houses. With burgundy thread, hand-stitch the

gold house to the green house using buttonhole stitch.

Step 7. Slip the assorted buttons on the craft wire. Wrap the wire around a pencil and give it many twists and curls. Glue or sew the ends to the eaves of the roof. Glue or sew a bow on each side over the ends of the wire. Place the potpourri packet in pocket on back of banner.

—By Debi Schmitz

Fig. 2
Stitch green square to back of house as shown.

Banner

Banner

Banner

Rug

Rug

Rug

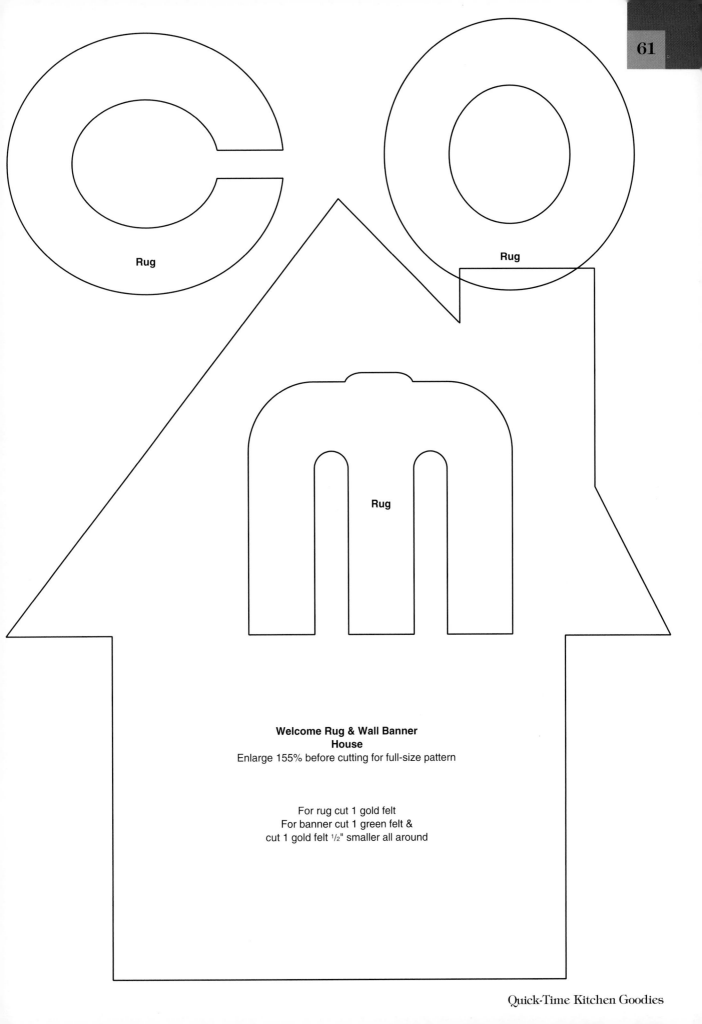

Rug

Rug

Rug

**Welcome Rug & Wall Banner
House**
Enlarge 155% before cutting for full-size pattern

For rug cut 1 gold felt
For banner cut 1 green felt &
cut 1 gold felt ¹/₂" smaller all around

Welcome to Our Roost

*A new morning, fresh farm eggs and a bright sun just coming over the hill—
anyone visiting your roost will crow about this warm welcome.*

Project Specifications

Skill Level: Intermediate
Banner Size: Approximately 8½" x 20"

Materials

- ⅓ yard background fabric
- ⅓ yard backing fabric
- ⅛ yard inner border
- ⅛ yard outer border
- Variety of scraps for appliqué
- 14 small buttons
- All-purpose thread to match fabric
- 6-strand green embroidery floss
- Gold metallic thread
- ⅓ yard thin batting
- Scraps of fusible transfer web
- Basic sewing supplies and tools

Instructions

Step 1. Use pattern to cut background piece.

Step 2. Trace appliqué shapes for rooster, sun and cloud onto paper side of fusible transfer web; cut out leaving roughly ½" margin around shapes.

Step 3. Fuse to wrong side of selected fabrics according to manufacturer's directions and cut out on tracing line.

Step 4. Position appliqué pieces. For easy placement, tape pattern sheet to windowpane with background piece on top. Pin appliqué pieces in place. Trace letters, flowers, sun rays and chicken feet. Fuse appliqué pieces.

Step 5. Cut batting 1½" larger than background piece. Place under background piece and pin in place.

Step 6. Satin-stitch around each appliqué piece and around lettering.

Step 7. From inner border fabric cut bias strip 1" x 30" (piece if not long enough) and straight-grain strip 1" x 20". Right sides together, pin bias strip around arch and stitch. Press up over batting and trim. Repeat with straight strip across bottom.

Step 8. Repeat Step 6 but with outer border fabric.

Step 9. Trim batting to size of finished piece.

Step 10. With gold metallic thread, hand-quilt sun rays. With one strand of floss, straight-stitch flower stems. Embroider leaves as desired with lazy-daisy stitch. Stitch buttons in place for flowers. (Try making tiny yo-yos for some flowers.)

Step 11. Place piece on backing and use as pattern to cut. Place right sides together and beginning off-center at bottom stitch with ¼" seam allowance. Stitch around periphery, leaving enough open for turning. Turn right side out and close opening by hand.

Step 12. Quilt in the ditch along border seams and close to outside edge.

—By Sandy Dye

Welcome to Our Roost
Enlarge 180% before cutting for full-size patterns

Casserole Carrier

Enclose a baking dish of the appropriate size, several of your favorite recipes, and this keep-it-warm carrier makes a great gift for almost any occasion.

Project Specifications

Skill Level: Beginner

Casserole Carrier Size: Approximately 12" diameter for 1½-quart covered casserole.

Note: *To accommodate casserole of a different size, measure covered casserole as shown in Fig. 1 and add 2". That measurement becomes the diameter of the circle to cut for the casserole carrier.*

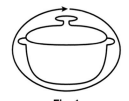

Fig. 1
Measure casserole as shown and add 2" for circle diameter.

Materials

- 26" squares of 2 coordinating 100 percent cotton fabrics
- 26" square fusible fleece or old ironing board cover
- 26" square insulated fleece or batting (has a shiny metallic finish on one side)
- 2 yards cotton cording
- 1 package contrasting maxi piping
- Chalk marker
- All-purpose thread to match fabrics
- Basic sewing supplies and tools

Instructions

Step 1. Cut a 26" circle of each cotton fabric. Cut a 25" circle of fusible fleece and insulated fleece.

Step 2. Center and bond fusible-fleece circle to wrong side of one fabric circle, following manufacturer's directions. This will be the outer shell. Stitch piping around the periphery.

Step 3. Center insulated fleece on wrong side of remaining fabric circle with shiny side toward fabric; baste in place around periphery.

Step 4. Draw a line 1" away from periphery of bonded circle with chalk marker. Draw another line ⅞" away from first line as shown in Fig. 2. Work two ⅝" buttonholes inside those lines, as shown in Fig. 3.

Step 5. Place backed fabric circles together, right sides facing. Stitch around the periphery with a ½" seam allowance, leaving an opening for turning.

Step 6. Clip curves; turn right side out. Close opening with a hand-sewing needle and thread.

Step 7. Stitch along chalk lines through all layers to create a casing.

Step 8. Cut cotton cording in half. Feed one piece through one buttonhole, around the casing and back out through the same buttonhole, as in Fig. 4. Tie ends of cord together in a knot. Feed remaining cord through other buttonhole, around casing and back out through the same buttonhole. Tie ends of cord together in a knot.

Step 9. Place covered casserole inside carrier; pull knotted ends of cords to fit the carrier around the casserole.

—By Beth Wheeler

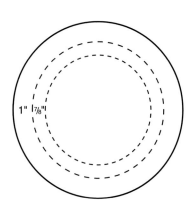

Fig. 2
Draw lines around circle as shown.

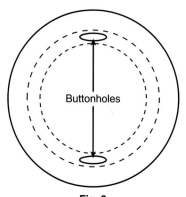

Fig. 3
Place buttonholes as shown.

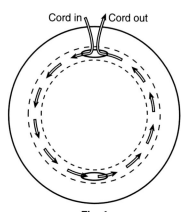

Fig. 4
Draw cord through casing as shown.

Fast and Fun Baby Gifts

Babies have their own timing. Fashionably late, or impishly early, they make an entrance when they are good and ready— proving who's really in charge! Early or late, the baby on the go will appreciate a comfy fleece bunting or blanket and Mom will love the whimsical diaper bags.

At home, the coordinating accessory set and sweet laundry bag will keep baby's room organized—and who would guess the beautiful christening gown began life as a pillowcase? Greet the new arrival with a welcome gift to be treasured for years to come.

Bear Baby Set

Teddy bears and hearts are favorite motifs in the nursery. This adorable pastel plaid ensemble handmade by you will delight new Baby and Mom. See photo on page 66.

Project Specifications

Skill Level: Beginner
Bib Size: Approximately 8" x 10"
Door Sign Size: Approximately 9" x 12"
Burp Cloth Size: Approximately 8" x 18½"
Growth Chart Size: Approximately 7" x 40"

Materials

- 1 yard cream print
- 1⅓ yards plaid
- Scraps of brown, blue and rose for appliqué
- ¼ yard fusible transfer web
- ⅛ yard tear-away fabric stabilizer
- ⅔ yard fleece
- Rayon machine-embroidery thread to match appliqué pieces
- All-purpose thread to match fabrics
- 1 package cream baby rickrack
- 1 package cream bias corded piping
- 1 package wide blue bias tape
- Black and rose 6-strand embroidery floss
- ¾ yard (⅜"-wide) rose grosgrain ribbon
- 1¼ yard (⅛"-wide) blue satin ribbon
- 3 (1") plastic O rings
- Polyester fiberfill
- 1 (60") white tape measure
- Glue gun
- Rotary-cutting tools
- Basic sewing supplies and tools

Instructions

Note: Use ¼" seam allowance unless otherwise indicated.

Bear Bib

Step 1. Cut bib pieces as directed on pattern.

Step 2. Trace bib top (above dashed line on pattern) on paper side of fusible web. Cut out leaving roughly ½" margin around shape. Place on the bias on wrong side of plaid fabric and fuse according to manufacturer's directions. Cut out on tracing lines. Fuse to top of cream bib front piece.

Step 3. Place fleece on wrong side of plaid bib back. Top with bib front right side up. Pin and topstitch all layers ⅛" from edge.

Step 4. Cut 8" length of rickrack. Center over straight division between plaid and cream areas of bib top. Topstitch in place. Cut a 25" length of rickrack and starting at top right of bib, topstitch in place around outer edge of bib ⅝" from edge.

Step 5. Cut one bias plaid strip 1¼" x 28" and one 1¼" x 33". Press one long edge under ¼" on each strip. Sew the long unpressed edge of the short strip around the outer edge of the bib. Turn the folded edge to the back, pin and hand-stitch in place.

Step 6. Find midpoint of longer tie and pin to center front of bib, matching raw edges. Pin and stitch around bib neckline. Turn folded edge to back and hand-stitch. Fold under raw edge of each tie ¼". Fold strip in half, pin and topstitch entire length.

Step 7. Trace appliqué pieces on paper side of fusible web. Cut out leaving roughly ½" margin around shapes. Using photo as a guide, fuse appliqué shapes to wrong sides of selected fabrics according to manufacturer's directions; cut out on tracing lines.

Step 8. Position shapes on bib and fuse in place. With a pencil, lightly draw face on bear and balloon string.

Step 9. Machine-appliqué with satin stitch and matching thread. Use straight stitch for balloon string. With rose thread, add decorative machine heart stitch at each X marked on the bear.

Step 10. With 4 strands of black embroidery floss make a French knot for each eye. With pink floss embroider nose and mouth. Tie a small bow from ⅛"-wide blue satin ribbon and stitch in place marked by A on pattern.

Burp Cloth

Step 1. Cut burp cloth pieces as directed on pattern.

Step 2. Trace burp cloth pattern on paper side of fusible web, except for lower front section of one end below dashed line as shown in Fig. 1. Cut out leaving roughly ½" margin around shape. Place on the bias on wrong side of plaid fabric and fuse according to manufacturer's directions. Cut out on tracing lines. Fuse to cream burp cloth piece to make top.

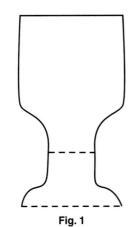

Fig. 1
Trace pattern except for lower front section of one end below dashed line.

Step 3. Place fleece on wrong side of plaid back. Place wrong side of top over fleece. Topstitch layers together ⅛" from edge.

Step 4. Cut 50" length of rickrack and topstitch around entire burp cloth ⅝" from outer edge. Cut an 8" length of rickrack, center and topstitch over straight division between plaid and cream areas on burp cloth top.

Step 5. Cut a 1¼" x 55" bias strip of plaid. Press one long edge under ¼". Sew raw edge of bias strip around edge of burp cloth. Turn pressed edge to back and hand-stitch in place.

Step 6. Complete bear appliqué following Steps 7–10 of bib instructions.

Door Sign

Step 1. Cut two cream print rectangles and one fleece 6¼" x 9¼". Place fleece between wrong sides of cream print rectangles; pin. Topstitch ⅛" from outer edge.

Step 2. Follow Step 7 of bib for appliqué pieces. Center bear vertically and 1¼" from left side of cream rectangle; fuse. With pencil, lightly write the words, "Shhh! Baby's Sleeping," referring to photo for position.

Step 3. Complete bear appliqué following bib Steps 8–10. Machine straight stitch the written words in rose thread. Use 2 strands of rose embroidery floss to make French knots to dot the i and exclamation mark.

Step 4. Sew piping around outside of appliquéd rectangle, overlapping ends. Clip piping before stitching around corners for smoother turn.

Step 5. Cut a 12" length of rose grosgrain. Center each end of ribbon 2" from each corner at top of appliquéd rectangle for hanger; topstitch.

Step 6. Cut a 4" x 45" plaid strip for ruffle. Sew short ends together. Fold strip in half lengthwise; press. Sew a basting stitch around raw edges. Pull to gather strip to fit around appliquéd rectangle; pin and stitch.

Step 7. Cut a 6¼" x 9¼" plaid rectangle for sign back. With right sides together and making sure ruffle does not get caught in seam, sew the front and back together leaving a 3" opening for turning. Trim corners and turn right side out. Stuff lightly with polyester fiberfill. Hand-stitch the opening closed.

Step 8. Tie two small bows from rose grosgrain ribbon. Hand-stitch a bow to each end of hanging loop on front of door sign.

Baby Bear Set
Growth Chart
Heart

Continued on page 85

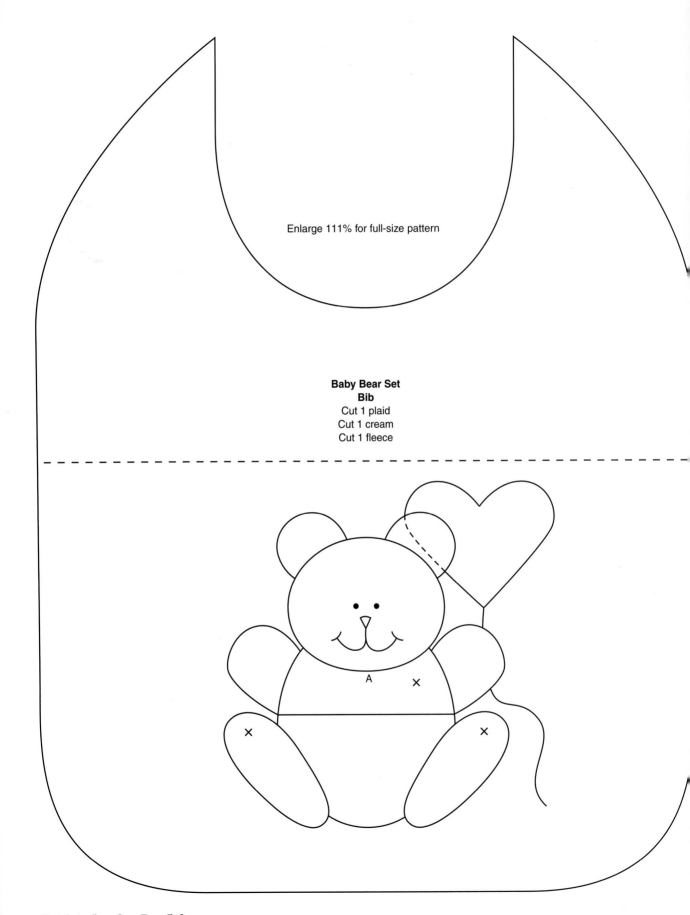

Enlarge 111% for full-size pattern

Baby Bear Set
Bib
Cut 1 plaid
Cut 1 cream
Cut 1 fleece

A

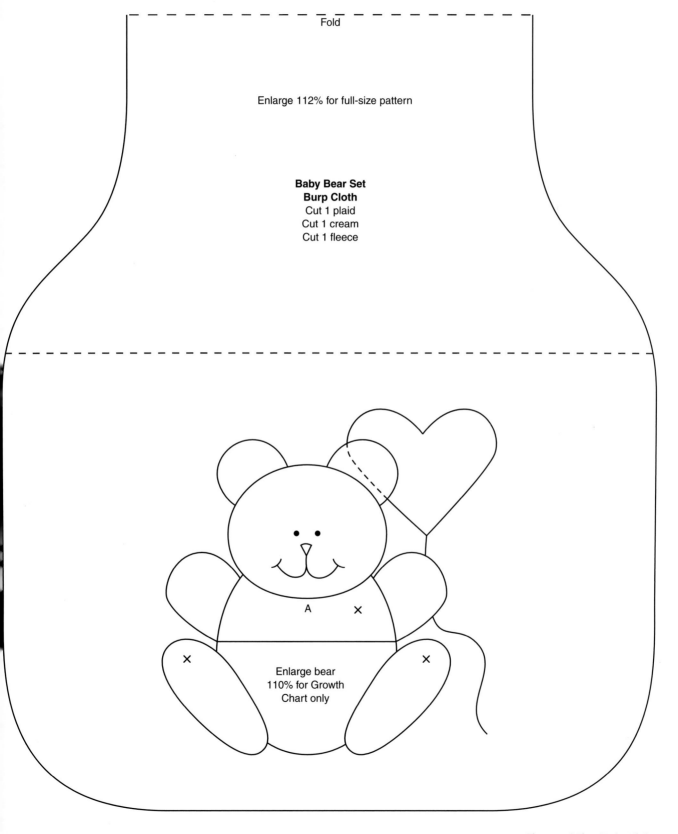

Fold

Enlarge 112% for full-size pattern

Baby Bear Set
Burp Cloth
Cut 1 plaid
Cut 1 cream
Cut 1 fleece

A

Enlarge bear
110% for Growth
Chart only

Baby Bunting

Fleece is a very forgiving fabric and so easy to work with, you'll enjoy adapting any baby sweatshirt or sleepwear pattern to make this soft, snugly bunting.

Project Specifications

Skill Level: Beginner

Bunting Size: Any infant size

Materials

Note: Most fleece fabric is not approved for sleepwear. Therefore, this bunting should only be used as outerwear.

Our sample is made to fit a baby 27"–28" long, 16–18 pounds. Adjust fabric and zipper accordingly.

- Any commercial infant sweatshirt or sleepwear pattern
- 1 yard fleece fabric
- ¼ yard tubular cotton ribbing
- 22" zipper
- All-purpose thread to match fabric
- Tracing paper
- Basic sewing supplies and tools

Instructions

Step 1. Place tracing paper over front and back pieces of commercial pattern. Redraw sides and bottom edges to make a simple bag shape as shown by dotted lines in Fig. 1.

Step 2. Using redrawn pattern pieces, cut one back, two fronts (reversing one) and two sleeves (reversing one).

Step 3. Baste center front seam to accommodate zipper length. Stitch remainder of seam with ⅝" seam allowance and regular stitch. Insert zipper, following package directions. Remove basting threads.

Step 4. Stitch front and back together with ⅝" seam allowance.

Step 5. Measure wrist edge of sleeve. Cut two pieces of ribbing ¾ that length plus 1¼" (seam allowances) x 4" with ribs running vertically as shown in Fig. 2.

Step 6. Fold ribbing in half lengthwise; stitch one ribbing cuff to each sleeve, stretching slightly to fit. Stitch underarm seam. Insert sleeves in bunting.

Step 7. Measure distance around bunting neck. Cut a

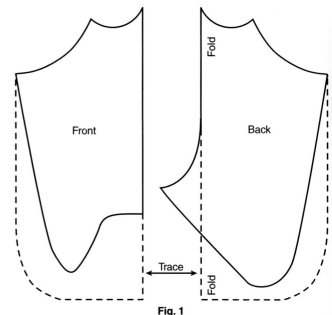

Fig. 1
Redraw sides and bottom of pattern to make bag shape.

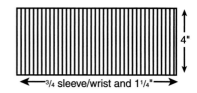

Fig. 2
Cut 4" vertical ribbing ¾ wrist edge length plus 1¼".

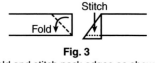

Fig. 3
Fold and stitch neck edges as shown to finish.

piece of ribbing ¾ that length plus 1¼" (for finished ends) x 3" with ribs running vertically.

Step 8. Stitch ribbing on neck edge, stretching gently to fit. Fold ends down as shown in Fig. 3. Stitch as indicated.

—By Beth Wheeler

Tumbling Blocks Blanket

Not only warm and fuzzy, but so fast and easy that, while you're at it, you may want to make several of these blankets to ensure always having a baby gift on hand.

Project Specifications

Skill Level: Beginner
Blanket Size: 36" x 36"

Materials

- 36" x 36" yellow fleece square
- Scraps of yellow, light and dark blue, light and dark pink, purple, orange and green fabrics
- 2 skeins mint green embroidery floss
- ¼ yard fusible transfer web
- ⅓ yard tear-away fabric stabilizer
- Rayon machine-embroidery thread to match fabric scraps
- White all-purpose thread
- Basic sewing supplies and tools

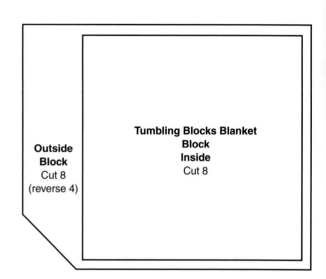

Outside Block
Cut 8
(reverse 4)

Tumbling Blocks Blanket Block Inside
Cut 8

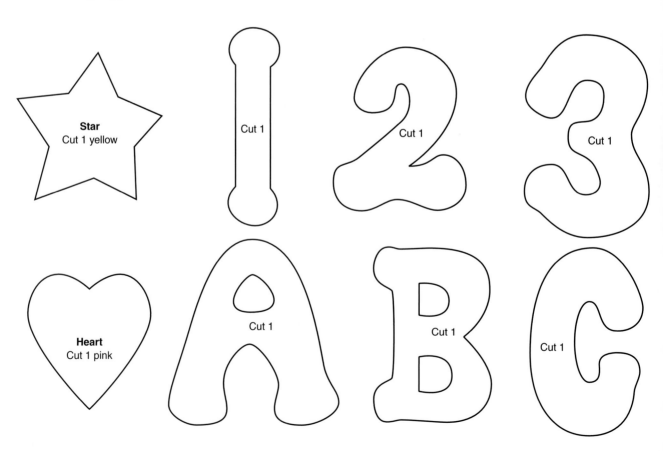

Star
Cut 1 yellow

Cut 1

Cut 1

Cut 1

Heart
Cut 1 pink

Cut 1

Cut 1

Cut 1

Instructions

Step 1. Use a salad plate to round off the corners of the fleece square.

Step 2. Trace appliqué shapes onto paper side of fusible transfer web as directed on patterns; cut out leaving roughly ½" margin around shapes.

Step 3. Fuse to wrong side of selected fabrics according to manufacturer's directions and cut out on tracing lines.

Step 4. Position appliqué pieces, referring to photo. With a pressing cloth over appliqué area, fuse in place.

Step 5. Pin tear-away fabric stabilizer behind appliqué area. Using all-purpose thread in the bobbin and rayon embroidery thread in the needle, satin-stitch around each appliqué, beginning with background pieces and working forward. Carefully tear away stabilizer.

Step 6. Using 6 strands of mint green embroidery floss, work buttonhole stitch around periphery of fleece (edges do not need to be turned under).

—By Leslie Hartsock

Dapper Diaper Bags

Mom can never have a diaper bag too large for the endless supplies necessary for traveling with baby. She'll thank you for making this oversized carryall!

Project Specifications

Skill Level: Intermediate
Diaper Bag Size: 17" x 15" x 6"

Materials

- 1 yard light-value fabric for background panels
- ⅓ yard darker-value fabric for lower front and back and gusset
- 1 yard coordinating print for lining and outer back pocket
- Scraps for hair, pacifier and hair bow
- 18" square skin-tone fabric
- 2¾ yards (1"-wide) woven webbing for handles
- 3 packages coordinating piping
- ⅔ yard fusible fleece
- Scraps of fusible transfer web
- 1" plastic ring for pacifier
- 1 (¾") shank button
- Rayon machine-embroidery thread to match appliqué fabrics
- Black and red permanent fabric markers
- All-purpose thread to match fabrics
- Basic sewing supplies and tools

Instructions

Step 1. For lower front and back cut two darker-value fabric rectangles 5" x 18". Cut two background panels from light-value fabric 12" x 18". Cut bottom gusset from darker-value print 7" x 18" and two side gussets 7" x 16". From lining fabric cut two outer back pocket pieces 10" x 11" and two inner pocket pieces 14" square. Cut two pieces for front and back lining 16" x 18", two gusset pieces 7" x 16" and one 7" x 18".

Step 2. Cut handle webbing in two equal pieces. Position ends of one piece on right side of one background panel as shown in Fig. 1. Stitch across lower ends ½" from bottom.

Step 3. Stitch piping along one long edge of front lower piece. Stitch front panel and lower piece together.

Step 4. Cut two fusible fleece 15" x 17". Fleece is cut smaller than corresponding fabric to reduce bulk in

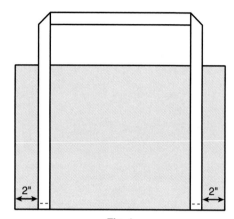

Fig. 1
Position ends of handle as shown.
Stitch across lower ends ½" from bottom.

seams. Center and fuse one piece to wrong side of front. Topstitch close to edges of handle webbing, stopping 1" from top edge of background piece as shown in Fig. 2.

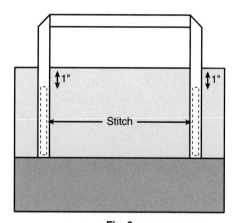

Fig. 2
Topstitch close to edges of handle
webbing, stopping 1" from top edge.

Step 5. Trace appliqué shapes onto paper side of fusible transfer web; cut out leaving roughly ½" margin around shapes.

Step 6. Referring to photo, fuse to wrong side of selected fabrics according to manufacturer's directions; cut out on tracing line.

Step 7. Position appliqué pieces and fuse in place. Satin-stitch around each appliqué piece with matching thread.

Step 8. Stitch piping along one long edge of one outer

78

back pocket piece. Place pocket pieces together with right sides facing. Stitch along one side of pocket, across top with piping and down the other side. Trim corners, turn right side out; press.

Step 9. Stitch handles on remaining background panel as in Step 2. Stitch piping as in Step 3. Position pocket on background panel between handles and with raw edges even. Baste through all layers close to raw edges. Stitch top panel and bottom piece together, right sides facing.

Step 10. Center and fuse remaining piece of fleece to wrong side of back unit. Topstitch close to both sides of handles as in Step 4. Topstitch close to edges of pocket, leaving top open. Topstitch down center of pocket to divide in two sections.

Step 11. Stitch piping around sides and bottom of front and back sections.

Step 12. Stitch gusset pieces as shown in Fig. 3. Press seams open. Cut fusible fleece 6" x 47" (to piece length, butt ends together). Center and fuse to wrong side of gusset.

Step 13. Stitch front and back sections together with gusset between. Stitch piping around top edge.

7" x 16"	7" x 18"	7" x 16"

Fig. 3
Stitch gusset pieces together as shown.

Lining

Step 1. Stitch lining gusset together as shown in Fig. 3.

Step 2. Stitch inner pocket pieces together along three sides. Trim corners, turn right side out; press. Position

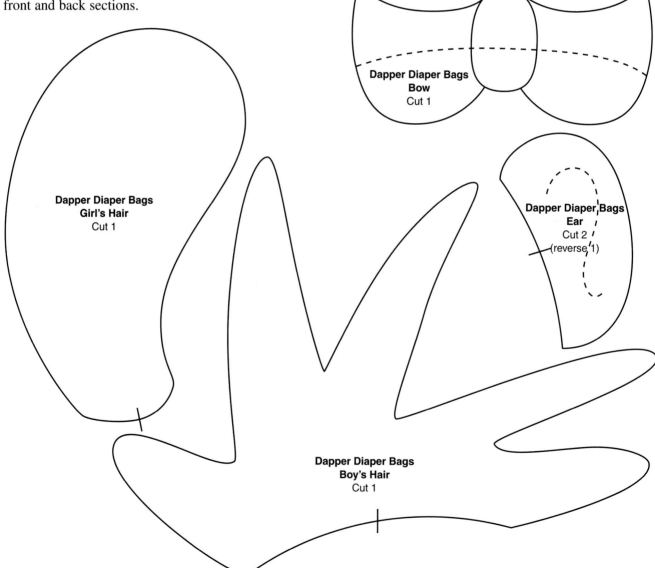

Dapper Diaper Bags
Bow
Cut 1

Dapper Diaper Bags
Girl's Hair
Cut 1

Dapper Diaper Bags
Ear
Cut 2
(reverse 1)

Dapper Diaper Bags
Boy's Hair
Cut 1

even with bottom edge of one lining piece. Topstitch close to sides and bottom of pocket.

Step 3. Stitch lining front and back sections together with gusset between.

Step 4. Place bag inside lining, right sides together. Stitch around top, leaving an opening for turning. Trim corners; turn right side out through opening. Close opening.

Finishing

Step 1. Fold back at each bottom and side seam and topstitch through all layers close to edge. This helps the bag hold its shape and stand, empty or full. Topstitch around top of bag through handles and all layers as shown in Fig. 4. Stitch an X in a box at the top of each handle to reinforce.

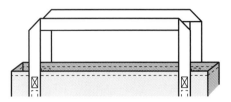

Fig. 4
Topstitch around top of bag and secure handles as shown.

Step 2. Add eyes, eyebrows and smile with black permanent fabric marker. Rub red permanent fabric marker on your index finger and immediately rub in a circular motion on cheek areas. Repeat for desired intensity.

Note: Features may be embroidered if desired.

Step 3. Stitch plastic ring and button in place for pacifier.

—By Beth Wheeler

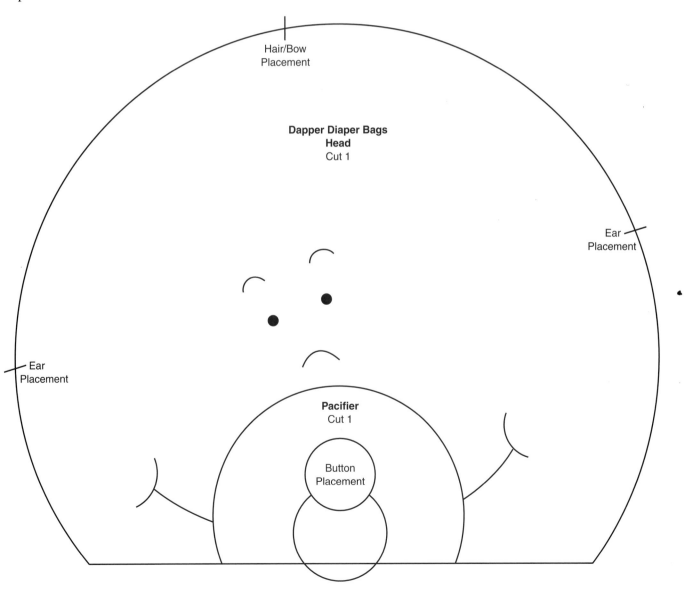

Hair/Bow
Placement

**Dapper Diaper Bags
Head
Cut 1**

Ear
Placement

Ear
Placement

**Pacifier
Cut 1**

Button
Placement

Christening Gown

Simply sweet and charming, and what a surprise! This lovely little christening gown emerged from a simple ready-made pillowcase. What could be easier?

Project Specifications

Skill Level: Beginner

Christening Gown Size: Infant

Materials

- Baby dress pattern, such as McCalls 2022
- Pillowcase with decorative eyelet edge
- ¼ yard white eyelet for bodice and sleeves
- ¼ yard white batiste for lining
- Package of piping to match pillowcase trim
- Package of single-fold white bias tape
- All-purpose thread to match fabrics
- Basic sewing supplies and tools

Instructions

Step 1. Cut one bodice and two sleeves each from eyelet and batiste. Assemble bodice and lining separately.

Step 2. Stitch piping around neckline and bottom of bodice. Place lining and bodice right sides together. Stitch around neckline; turn right side out.

Step 3. Stitch underarm seam of each sleeve and lining. Work a gathering stitch around lower edge of eyelet sleeve; pull to gather. Stitch piping around opening. Gather lower edges of sleeve linings to match sleeves. Place sleeve and lining right sides together. Stitch together along piping edge. Fold lining up to encase raw edges.

Step 4. Work gathering stitch along sleeve cap and lining. Set sleeves into bodice. Bind raw edges of seam with bias tape.

Step 5. Remove stitches from closed end of pillowcase. Work a running stitch around the opened edge. Gather to fit lower edge of bodice.

Step 6. Stitch bodice (not lining) and skirt together with right sides facing. Press seam allowance toward bodice. Slipstitch lining to seam.

Step 7. Finish back opening according to dress pattern directions, stitching buttons and buttonholes.

—*By Beth Wheeler*

Laundry Bag Bear

Laundry multiplies continually in the nursery, so having a cute way to handle the accumulation is half the battle. This little bear is prepared to help.

Project Specifications

Skill Level: Beginner
Laundry Bag Size: 18" x 24"

Materials

- 1½ yards 72"-wide pink felt
- ½ yard white felt
- ⅓ yard plaid flannel
- 1 pair (42 mm) comical eyes
- 3 (¾") white buttons
- White all-purpose thread
- White pearl cotton
- White plastic coat hanger
- Craft glue
- Basic sewing supplies and tools

Instructions

Step 1. Cut four 18" x 24" pieces of pink felt. Stack them together and place coat hanger across one end. Trim felt to fit hanger as shown in Fig. 1.

Step 2. Cut plaid flannel and felt as directed on patterns.

Step 3. Referring to photo, machine-stitch nose, cheeks and body flannel pieces onto corresponding felt pieces.

Step 4. Stitch pink felt ears, nose, cheeks and top of eyelids (leave straight edge unstitched) to head.

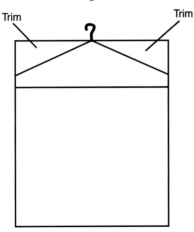

Fig. 1
Trim felt to fit hanger as shown.

Step 5. Layer two pieces of pink felt for bag front. Sew body onto bag. Angle head and sew it to body, slightly overlapping body. Stitch paws in place. With pearl cotton work buttonhole stitch around all appliqué pieces.

Step 6. Cut a plaid flannel strip 2" x 28". Tie a bow and stitch to neck of bear. Sew buttons on front of body. Glue eyes in place (may need to cut off shank to glue flat) and buttonhole-stitch lower edge of eyelid.

Step 7. Layer two back felt pieces. Make a 10" vertical cut 4" from top as shown in Fig. 2. With pearl cotton, work buttonhole stitch around opening.

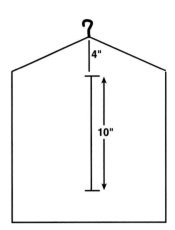

Fig. 2
Make a vertical cut in bag back as shown.

Step 8. Place front and back piece together, pin and trim. Work buttonhole stitch around periphery. Stitch top front and back separately at center top to slip hanger through.

Step 9. Insert hanger and hang in closet or on door for laundry.

—By Debi Schmitz

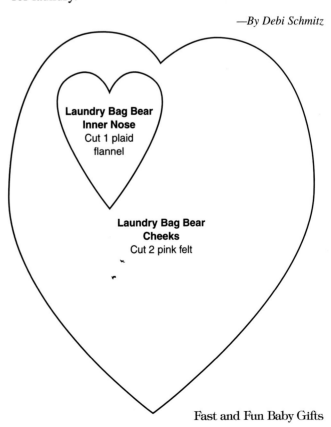

Laundry Bag Bear
Inner Nose
Cut 1 plaid flannel

Laundry Bag Bear
Cheeks
Cut 2 pink felt

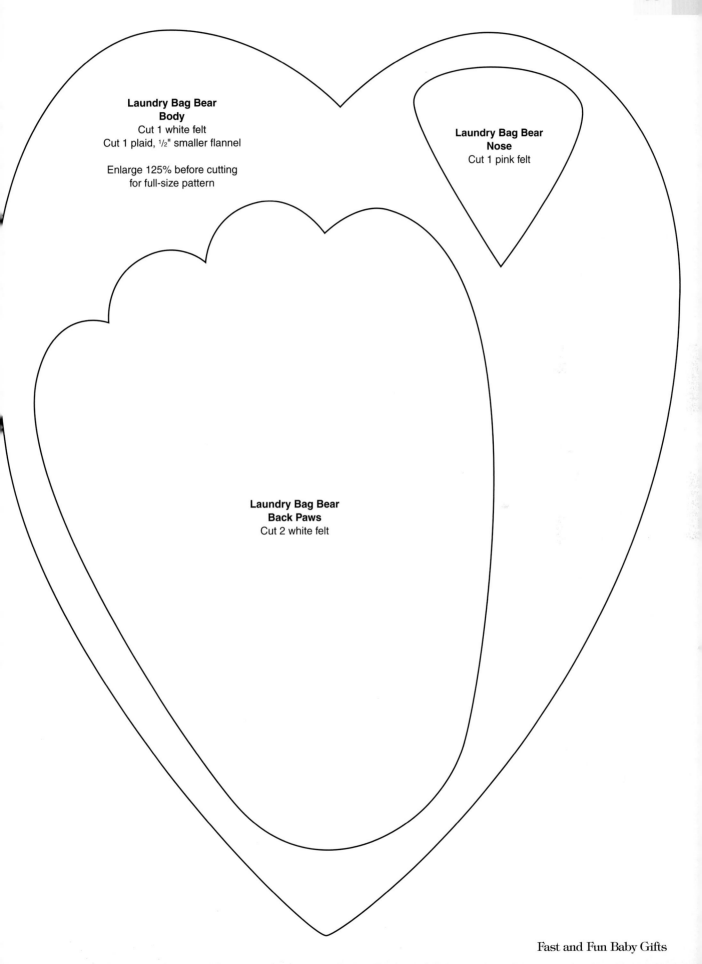

**Laundry Bag Bear
Body**
Cut 1 white felt
Cut 1 plaid, 1/2" smaller flannel

Enlarge 125% before cutting
for full-size pattern

**Laundry Bag Bear
Nose**
Cut 1 pink felt

**Laundry Bag Bear
Back Paws**
Cut 2 white felt

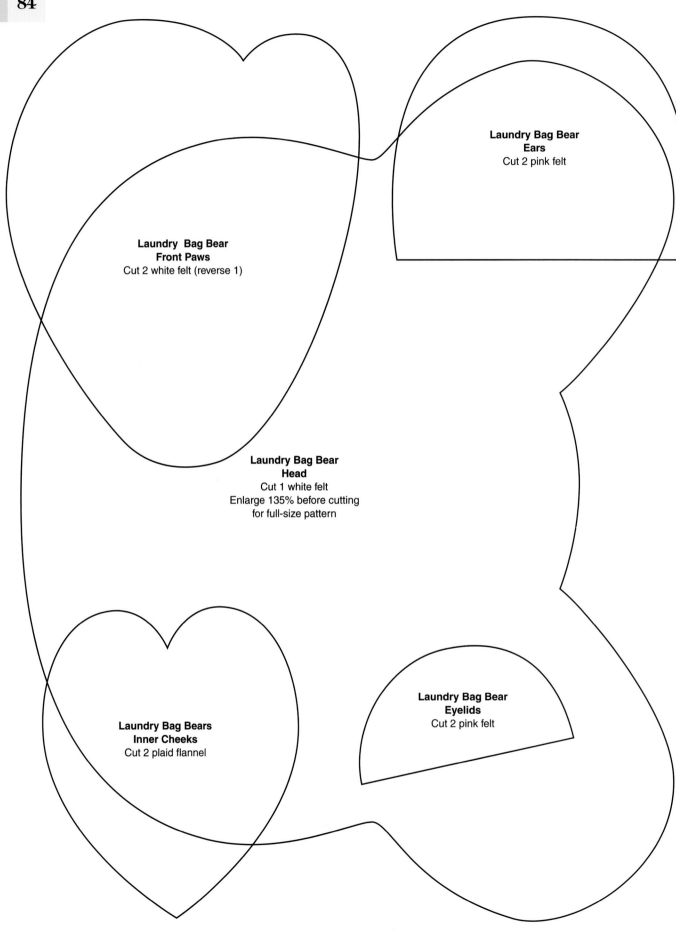

**Laundry Bag Bear
Ears**
Cut 2 pink felt

**Laundry Bag Bear
Front Paws**
Cut 2 white felt (reverse 1)

**Laundry Bag Bear
Head**
Cut 1 white felt
Enlarge 135% before cutting
for full-size pattern

**Laundry Bag Bears
Inner Cheeks**
Cut 2 plaid flannel

**Laundry Bag Bear
Eyelids**
Cut 2 pink felt

Baby Bear Set
Continued from page 69

Growth Chart

Step 1. Cut two 7½" x 40½" strips from cream print, one from plaid and one from fleece. Lightly draw a pencil line 1½" from right side down the length of the cream print strip.

Step 2. Using enlarged bear pattern, follow Step 7 of bib pattern. Position bear 1½" from left edge and 3" up from bottom; fuse.

Step 3. Measure 3" above center top of bear. Lightly make a pencil dot. Position bottom point of large heart pattern on dot. Trace around heart. Measure 3" above center of heart and make a dot. Position heart pattern again and trace. Repeat until five hearts are traced. Lightly draw a pencil line under each heart for a "balloon string." Carefully cut out each traced heart.

Step 4. Cut five 4" squares from stabilizer and center one behind each cut-out heart; pin. Machine-appliqué a satin stitch around the raw edge of each heart. Topstitch balloon strings. Carefully remove the stabilizer pieces.

Step 5. Center fleece strip on remaining cream strip. Center wrong side of plaid strip on top of fleece and appliquéd strip on top of plaid. Plaid will show through hearts.

Step 6. Pin and topstitch layers together ⅛" from outer edges. Pin around each heart and topstitch ⅛" from edge. This will form an opening in which to insert a photo in each heart.

Step 7. Follow bib Steps 9 and 10 to complete bear appliqué.

Step 8. Tie five small bows from blue ribbon. Stitch a bow at the point of each heart balloon.

Step 9. Bind with blue bias tape. Add three plastic O rings to back of top edge for hanging.

Step 10. With 60" mark at top of Growth Chart, use glue gun to glue measuring tape to line marked in Step 1. Trim tape at bottom of chart.

Step 11. Instruct recipient to mark measuring dates with ultra-fine permanent marker and to cut and glue annual photos in plaid heart spaces.

—By Michele Crawford

It's Never Too Late For Dolls And Toys

Who says dolls and toys are just for kids? The charm of a chubby sock angel or shaggy stuffed chenille buddy can make anyone smile. The sewing dolls in this chapter are adorable and can lend a hand to your favorite sewing enthusiast. And what country collection would be complete without a lacy angel or snuggly snowman? From practical teaching toys to fantasy stick horses, knowing the pleasure a handcrafted doll can bring makes giving as wonderful as receiving!

Sock Angel Ornament

*You'll demonstrate how very much you care when you create one of these
pretty little angels to hover peacefully in a friend's home. See photo on page 86.*

Project Specifications

Skill Level: Beginner
Ornament Size: Approximately 6"

Materials

- 3 white newborn (0–6 months) tube socks
- 1 (¼") wooden button for nose
- 1⅔ yards (2½"-wide) pink iridescent wire-edged ribbon
- 1 yard (⅜"-wide) pink iridescent ribbon
- 1 tuft tightly curled white hair
- Gold adjustable craft wedding band
- ¼ yard gold cord for hanging loop
- Fabric glue
- Pink, black and white acrylic paint
- Air-drying disappearing marker
- Polyester fiberfill
- White all-purpose thread
- Powdered blush
- Cotton swab
- 5" doll needle
- Basic sewing supplies and tools

Instructions

Step 1. For the body, cut cuff off one sock and discard cuff. Sew gathering thread along cut edge, stuff firmly with polyester fiberfill, pull gathers tight and knot.

Step 2. To form head insert 5" doll needle with knotted thread 1½" down from center of toe seam of body. Wrap thread around sock twice. Pull thread tight and knot.

Step 3. For legs, cut cuff off one sock and discard cuff. From cut edge, cut one 1½" piece and put aside for arm. Run a gathering stitch along raw edge. Stuff firmly with polyester fiberfill, pull gathers tight and knot. To form foot insert doll needle with knotted thread 1" from toe seam, wrap thread twice around leg, pulling tight to indent; knot thread. Repeat for other leg and foot.

Step 4. To attach legs, insert doll needle with knotted thread 1" above bottom of body, through one side of body to other side, then through one leg. Insert needle back through same leg, through body and through other leg. Repeat twice, pulling thread tight. Insert needle through one leg and bring needle out between leg and body; knot thread.

Step 5. To make arms, run a gathering stitch along one raw edge of one arm piece. Pull thread tight and knot. Run a gathering stitch along other raw edge, pull gathers slightly and firmly stuff with polyester fiberfill. For hands, insert needle ½" from one raw edge. Wrap thread twice around arm, pulling tight to indent; knot thread. Repeat for other arm and hand.

Step 6. Paint ¼" wooden button pink. When dry, glue nose to face. Paint two black dots for eyes and a white comma stroke on the nose. Blush cheeks with powdered blush and cotton swab.

Step 7. Cut ⅔ yard of 2½"-wide iridescent pink wire-edged ribbon and put aside for skirt. Center remaining ribbon at bodice front and wrap around to back and tie, leaving ribbon tails free.

Step 8. With skirt ribbon, pull out wire from one edge of ribbon. Pulling on both wire ends of other edge of ribbon gather skirt to 4". Wrap around body at waist, with ends in back and under bodice ribbon tails. Twist ends of wire to secure; cut ends.

Step 9. Tie bodice ribbon tails in a bow to create wings. Trim ends of ribbon at an angle. Glue or sew one arm to each side of bodice. Tie two small bows with ⅜"-wide pink iridescent ribbon and glue to each leg. Tie one larger bow and glue to neck.

Step 10. Glue tuft of hair to top of head. For halo, separate wedding band ends slightly and glue to back of head angled to the side. Thread needle with gold cord and take a small stitch at top of head. Remove needle and knot ends of cord for hanging loop.

—By Veleta "Sam" Stafney

Sock Angel Doll

This little cherub is soft and cuddly and has feminine charm to share—from her perfect little rosebud-trimmed halo to her sweet little pink button nose. See photo on page 86.

Project Specifications

Skill Level: Beginner

Doll Size: Approximately 14"

Materials

- ¼ yard pastel plaid fabric
- 3 pairs boy's small (3–11½ shoe size) white tube socks
- 2¼ yards (½"-wide) white ruffled lace
- ⅓ yard (1⅜"-wide) pink iridescent ribbon
- 2 (6") puffy angel wings
- 12" white pine stem
- ½ yard (3mm) pink pearl strand
- 1 (1") pink double rosebud
- 4 (¾") white buttons
- 1 (⅜") wooden button for nose
- 2 (9mm) black half-round ball eyes
- Polyester fiberfill
- White all-purpose thread
- White pearl cotton
- Fabric glue
- Pink and white acrylic paint
- Toothpick
- Powdered blush
- Cotton swab
- 5" doll needle
- Basic sewing supplies and tools

Instructions

Doll

Step 1. For body, cut cuff off one sock; discard cuff. Turn wrong side out and stuff firmly with polyester fiberfill. Run basting stitch along raw edge, pull gathers tight and knot.

Step 2. For head, cut 4½" off cuff edge and along toe seam of one sock and discard cuts. Run a basting stitch along one raw edge. Pull gathers tight and knot. Turn wrong side out and stuff firmly. Run a basting stitch along other raw edge, pull gathers tight and knot thread. Pin one gathered edge of head to top of gathered edge of body. Hand-sew or glue head to gathered edge of body.

Step 3. For legs, cut off cuff and along toe seam of one sock and discard cuts. Run a basting stitch along one raw edge. Pull gathers tight and knot. Turn wrong side out and stuff firmly. Run a gathering stitch along other raw edge, pull gathers tight and knot. Repeat for other leg.

Step 4. For arms, cut 4" off cuff edge and along toe seam of one sock and discard. Finish each arm same as legs in Step 3.

Step 5. Thread 5" doll needle with long strand of pearl cotton and knot ends together. Insert needle 1" from bottom of body through one side of body to other side, then through one leg, one hole in button, back through other hole in button, through leg, back through body and through other leg and through one hole in another button. Repeat, pulling thread tight, twice, finally pulling needle out between leg and body; knot thread.

Step 6. Repeat step 5 for arms, attaching 1" from neck.

Step 7. Paint wooden button pink for nose. When dry, glue to face, referring to photo. With toothpick, make white comma stroke on nose.

Step 8. For eyes, thread 5" doll needle with pearl cotton and knot ends together. Insert needle from back of head at neck, coming out the front ½" above nose. Insert needle ⅛" over, back through head to neck, twice. Pull thread to indent eye area and knot thread in back at neck. Repeat for other eye. Cut eye stems off and glue eyes to eye indent.

Step 9. Blush cheeks with cotton swab and powdered blush.

Dress

Step 1. Cut a 4" x 42½" piece of pastel plaid fabric for skirt. Right sides facing, sew short ends together. Turn one long edge under ¼" for hem; press. Turn under again and press. Pin lace under hem and top-stitch in place.

Continued on page 91

Chenille Stick Horse

Every little tyke loves to ride and these ponies are so quick to make you may want a whole stable full to offer to the romping younger set. See photo on page 86.

Project Specifications

Skill Level: Beginner
Stick Horse Size: Approximately 41"

Materials

- ½ yard white chenille fabric
- Variety of ribbon and rickrack (1 yard each, 3 or 4 colors and sizes)
- Variety of yarn (2 yards each, 4 or 5 colors and textures)
- 15" (½"-wide) pink satin ribbon
- 4 yards (¼"-wide) pink-and-white gingham ribbon
- 8½" x 4½" tagboard or card stock
- Polyester fiberfill
- All-purpose thread to match chenille
- Tape
- 40" (1"-diameter) wooden dowel (or broom or tool handle)
- Pink spray paint
- 2 (1") blue buttons
- 2 (¾") silver Western-style buttons
- 2 white mini-tassels
- Craft glue
- Basic sewing supplies and tools

Instructions

Note: Use ¼" seam allowance unless otherwise noted.

Step 1. Wrap ribbons, rickrack and yarns around the 8½" side of tagboard strip, taping ends to secure at edges of board. Wrap each with spaces between and fill in as layers and textures build. The fuller the better, but not thicker than your machine will be able to sew through.

Step 2. Sew a straight stitch down one long side near the edge of the tagboard to secure all pieces together. With scissors, cut the edge not sewn so loops no longer exist. The machine stitch will have perforated the tagboard. Carefully pull it apart and discard.

Step 3. Trace and cut head pieces as directed on pattern. Using pattern as a guide, stitch pink-and-white gingham ribbon halter along each side of head (not nose).

Step 4. Fold the gusset piece lengthwise, right sides together. Place the stitched edge of mane into the fold between widest part of gusset and stitch a very narrow seam the length of the mane, making sure the mane is securely caught in the seam. (Mane will be down the center of the gusset piece.)

Step 5. Sew each pair of ears right sides together, leaving end open. Fold in half and stay-stitch open end. Sew one head piece to gusset, starting at back of neck and sewing toward inside of neck. Insert ear where marked, facing forward. Repeat with other side of head, starting at the same place.

Step 6. Sew button eyes in place. Stuff head area with polyester fiberfill, but not neck.

Step 7. Cut 12" piece of pink-and-white gingham ribbon. Hand-stitch one end to end of halter. Wrap completely around nose and hand-stitch to other end of halter.

Step 8. Cut 24" piece of pink-and-white gingham ribbon for reins. Hand-stitch ends to each end of halter. Cut loops on tassels and thread through silver buttons, tying in knot on button back. Sew one button in place over each end of rein.

Step 9. Spray at least two coats of pink paint on wooden dowel. Insert dowel through neck and to top of horse's head. Stuff evenly around dowel. Sew a gathering stitch around bottom neck edge. Before gathering, glue several inches of the inserted dowel to secure it to batting and prevent shifting. Pull gathering stitch until neck is tight against dowel. Secure and knot.

Step 10. Run a hand gathering stitch along one long edge of pink satin ribbon. Pull gathers to fit around neck end of dowel. Tighten, secure and knot. Add ribbon of glue around edge of chenille neck, slide gathered ribbon up and in place.

—By Kenna Prior

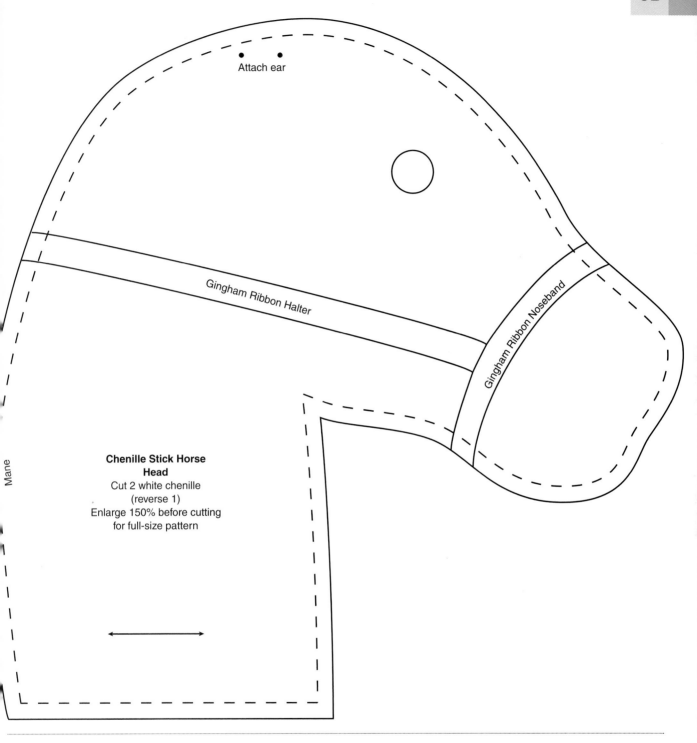

Attach ear

Gingham Ribbon Halter

Gingham Ribbon Noseband

Mane

Chenille Stick Horse Head
Cut 2 white chenille
(reverse 1)
Enlarge 150% before cutting
for full-size pattern

Sock Angel Doll

Continued from page 89

Step 2. Turn other long edge under ¼" and run basting stitch along fold. Place dress over body and pull gathers tight. Knot thread.

Step 3. Cut a 4" x 36" piece of pastel plaid for collar and finish same as for dress, pulling gathers tight around neck. With dot of glue, secure center back of collar to center back of doll.

Finishing

Step 1. For halo, bend white pine stem into a loop and twist ends to secure. Wrap pink pearl strand evenly around halo. Glue ends to hold. Place halo on top of head and glue or hand-sew to secure. Glue rosebud to side of halo.

Step 2. Tie a bow with 1⅜"-wide pink iridescent ribbon. Cut ends at angle. Glue bow to front of neck.

Step 3. Glue puffy angel wings to back of collar.

—By Veleta "Sam" Stafney

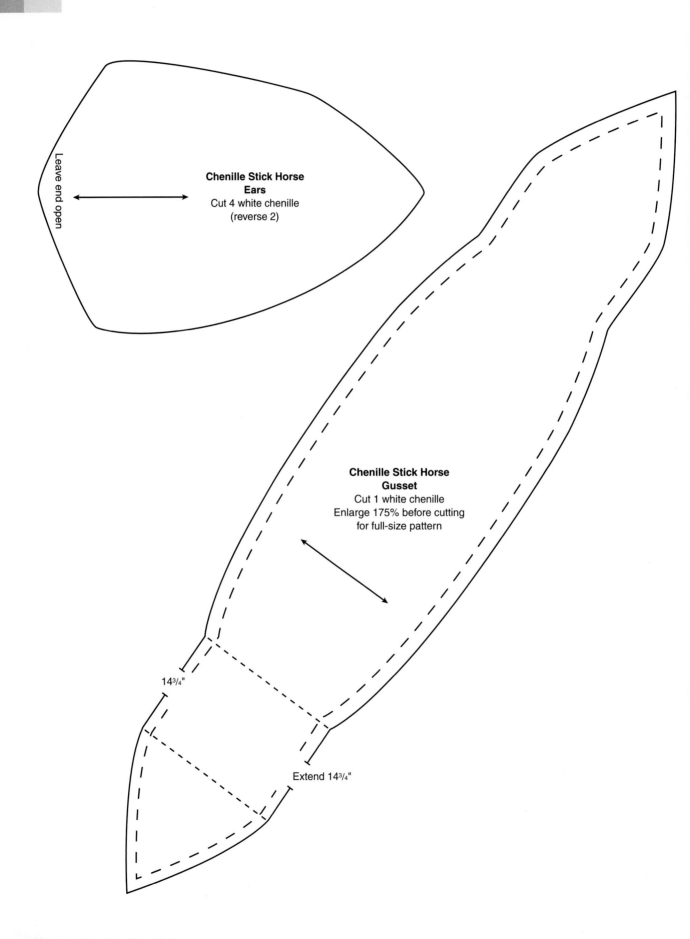

Leave end open

**Chenille Stick Horse
Ears**
Cut 4 white chenille
(reverse 2)

**Chenille Stick Horse
Gusset**
Cut 1 white chenille
Enlarge 175% before cutting
for full-size pattern

14³/₄"

Extend 14³/₄"

Chenille Teddy Bear

*Soft, snugly chenille is a perfect choice of fabric for this little bear,
who will be ready in moments to be someone's new best friend.*

Project Specifications

Skill Level: Beginner

Teddy Bear Size: Approximately 10"

Materials

- McCalls pattern 2272
- Cream chenille as required by pattern
- Cream and pale pink 6-strand embroidery floss
- Variety of pale pink and cream ribbons, beads, pearls and lace for embellishments
- 2 (¼") dark buttons or beads for eyes
- 4 (¾") wooden buttons for joints
- Pellet stuffing
- All-purpose thread to match chenille
- Basic sewing supplies and tools

Instructions

Step 1. Follow pattern for assembly.

Step 2. Add wooden buttons at joints.

Step 3. Sew eyes in place and embroider facial features.

Step 4. Embellish with trim as desired.

—By Kenna Prior

Sewing Doll

Too often the sewing room is "all business," but if you fashion this pretty lady for one of your sewing friends, you'll add a little whimsy to the atmosphere.

Project Specifications

Skill Level: Beginner

Doll Size: Approximately 16"

Materials

- 1 plastic 2-liter soda bottle
- ¼ yard white felt
- ½ yard floral-on-white fabric
- ½ yard green-and-white stripe fabric
- 1¼ yards (½"-wide) white ruffled eyelet lace
- 1 (6") white heart-shaped Battenburg lace doily
- ¼ yard (⅜"-wide) pink ribbon
- Blonde tightly curled doll hair
- 1 (2") wooden ball for head
- Wicker basket approximately ¾" x 2"
- Gold sewing scissors charm approximately 2"
- Variety of colors and sizes of buttons for basket
- 4 (⅝") pink buttons
- Polyester fiberfill
- 2 cups plastic pellets
- Flesh-tone and rose acrylic paint
- Black fine-point permanent marker
- All-purpose thread to match fabrics
- Cotton swab
- Glue gun or tacky glue
- Air-drying disappearing marker
- Basic sewing supplies and tools

Instructions

Note: Use ¼" seam allowance unless otherwise noted.

Step 1. Pour plastic pellets into bottle. Glue around inside of bottle cap and replace.

Step 2. Cut two pieces 8¼" x 13" from white felt. Round off corners on one edge of each piece as shown in Fig. 1. Pin felt together and sew both long side seams, leaving open at top and 3" along center bottom again referring to Fig. 1. Turn right side out. Run a basting stitch along both openings. Pull 3" opening gathers tight and knot. Slip bottle inside. Pull remaining gathers tight around neck of bottle and knot threads.

Fig. 1

3"

Step 3. Paint the wooden ball with flesh-tone acrylic paint. When dry, draw eyes, eyelashes and nose with permanent marker, referring to photo for placement. Apply blush to cheeks with cotton swab and rose acrylic paint. When dry, glue head to top of bottle cap.

Step 4. From floral-on-white fabric cut one piece 12½" x 42½" for dress. Sew short edges of dress piece together. Turn right side out. For hem, fold under one raw edge ¼"; press. Turn under again, press and stitch. Run a basting stitch along other raw edge. Place dress over bottle and pull gathers tight under neck of bottle. Knot threads and spot with glue to secure.

Step 5. From green-and-white stripe fabric cut one 12½" x 42½" piece. Sew short ends together and turn right side out. Fold under one raw edge ¼"; press. Turn under again and press. Pin eyelet lace under hem and topstitch. Measure 10½" intervals each side of back seam along hemline and mark with disappearing marker. Run a basting stitch along raw edge, place apron over dress and pull gathers tight under head. Knot threads and spot with glue to secure.

Step 6. At each previously marked 10½" segment of hem, run a 3½" running stitch perpendicular to hem as shown in Fig. 2. Pull gathers tight and knot. Sew one pink button over each gather.

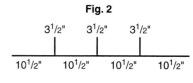

Fig. 2

3½" 3½" 3½"

10½" 10½" 10½" 10½"

Step 7. Cut a 5" x 15" piece of floral-on-white fabric for arms. Fold piece in half lengthwise and stitch. Turn right side out and run a basting stitch across arm center. Pull gathers tight and knot. Lightly stuff each arm (either side of gathers). Set aside.

Step 8. Cut a 2" square of floral fabric and fringe the edges ¼". Glue into basket. Arrange buttons and scissors in basket, gluing to hold in place. Place arms through basket handle. Overlap raw edges of both ends of arms and run a basting stitch through all layers. Pull gathers tight and knot. Place arms over head and glue ends to back of apron.

Step 9. Cut a slit in heart-shaped doily from point to

Continued on page 100

Shaggy Quilted Bunny

You'll love the nifty procedure of clipping, soaking and drying prequilted muslin to quickly achieve a great raggedy look for this adorable bunny rabbit.

Project Specifications

Skill Level: Beginner
Bunny Size: Approximately 21"

Materials

- 1 yard muslin prequilted in wave pattern, lines ¾" apart
- ¼ yard muslin
- 2 (12 mm) brown animal eyes
- ½ yard (1"-wide) cream ribbon
- Polyester fiberfill
- All-purpose cream thread
- Fabric glue
- Powder blush
- Cotton swab
- Basic sewing supplies and tools

Instructions

Note: Use ⅜" seam allowance unless otherwise noted. Raw edges are left on outside.

Step 1. Trace and cut bunny pieces as directed on patterns on pages 96–100.

Step 2. Stitch two arms and two legs together leaving openings as shown on pattern. On one body piece place arms and legs as shown in Fig. 1. (Sewn ends are placed within body, not open ends.) Place other body piece on top and pin to hold. Sew around body leaving top of head open.

Fig. 1

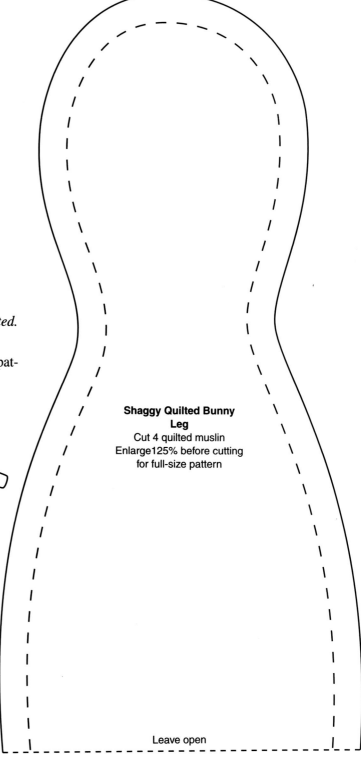

Shaggy Quilted Bunny Leg
Cut 4 quilted muslin
Enlarge 125% before cutting
for full-size pattern

Step 3. On both sides of body, arms and legs and on one side of ears, use pointed end of scissors to carefully poke through the top muslin and batting layer, but not through the bottom muslin layer. Cut a long slit through the two layers down the middle of each quilted area on each side of quilting line. Then cut perpendicular slits ⅜" apart as shown in Fig. 2. Do not cut through quilting lines.

Step 4. Thoroughly soak bunny and ears and dry

Leave open

Fig. 2

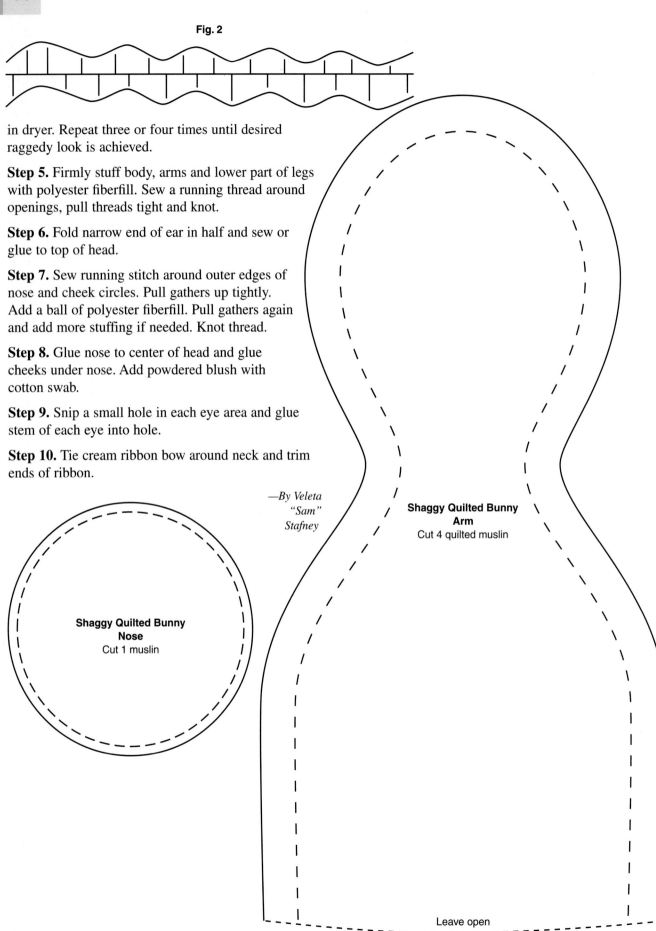

in dryer. Repeat three or four times until desired raggedy look is achieved.

Step 5. Firmly stuff body, arms and lower part of legs with polyester fiberfill. Sew a running thread around openings, pull threads tight and knot.

Step 6. Fold narrow end of ear in half and sew or glue to top of head.

Step 7. Sew running stitch around outer edges of nose and cheek circles. Pull gathers up tightly. Add a ball of polyester fiberfill. Pull gathers again and add more stuffing if needed. Knot thread.

Step 8. Glue nose to center of head and glue cheeks under nose. Add powdered blush with cotton swab.

Step 9. Snip a small hole in each eye area and glue stem of each eye into hole.

Step 10. Tie cream ribbon bow around neck and trim ends of ribbon.

—By Veleta "Sam" Stafney

Shaggy Quilted Bunny Nose
Cut 1 muslin

Shaggy Quilted Bunny Arm
Cut 4 quilted muslin

Leave open

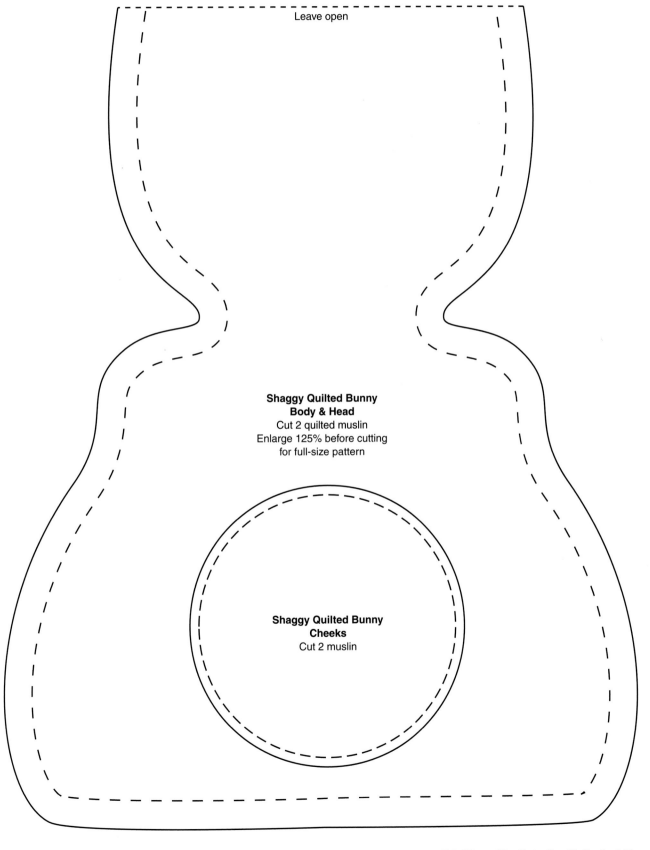

Leave open

**Shaggy Quilted Bunny
Body & Head**
Cut 2 quilted muslin
Enlarge 125% before cutting
for full-size pattern

**Shaggy Quilted Bunny
Cheeks**
Cut 2 muslin

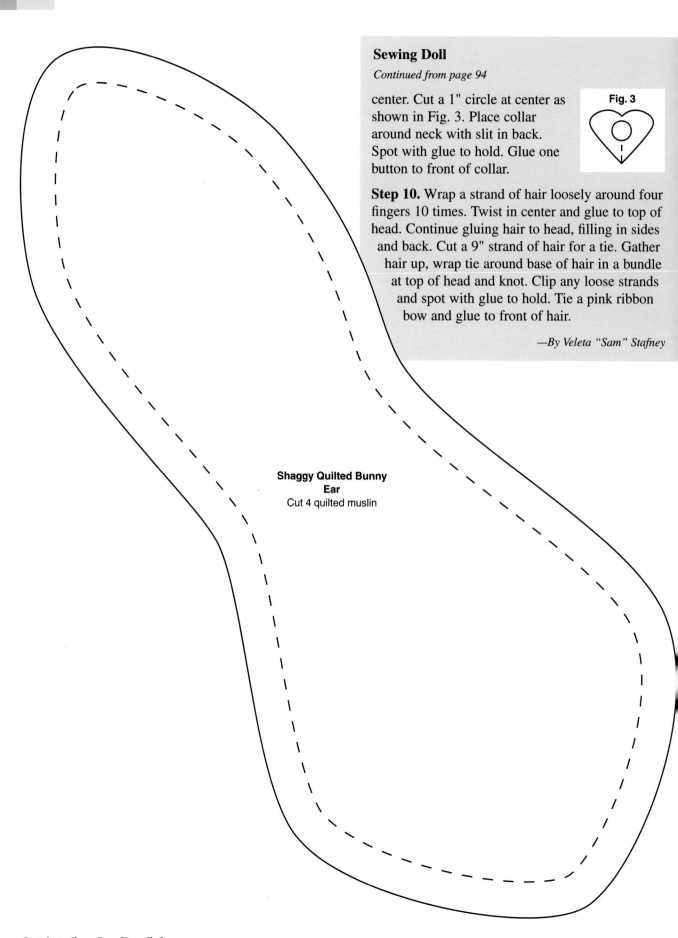

Sewing Doll

Continued from page 94

Fig. 3

center. Cut a 1" circle at center as shown in Fig. 3. Place collar around neck with slit in back. Spot with glue to hold. Glue one button to front of collar.

Step 10. Wrap a strand of hair loosely around four fingers 10 times. Twist in center and glue to top of head. Continue gluing hair to head, filling in sides and back. Cut a 9" strand of hair for a tie. Gather hair up, wrap tie around base of hair in a bundle at top of head and knot. Clip any loose strands and spot with glue to hold. Tie a pink ribbon bow and glue to front of hair.

—By Veleta "Sam" Stafney

Shaggy Quilted Bunny Ear
Cut 4 quilted muslin

Snowman Doll

This little guy is capped, dressed in his plaid woollies and sweater, muffled up to his eyeballs and just waiting patiently for a winter snowstorm!

Project Specifications

Skill Level: Beginner

Snowman Doll Size: Approximately 10" tall

Materials

- 12" x 8" white plush felt for body
- 16" x 8" plaid flannel for pants
- 6" x 7" black fabric for feet
- 2½" x 24" yellow felt for scarf
- 1 women's-size navy-blue sock
- 2 (10 mm) black shank buttons for eyes
- 1 (⅜") red shank button for nose
- 2 snow-theme novelty buttons
- 1 (½") blue button
- Black and white 6-strand embroidery floss
- Polyester fiberfill
- ¾ cup pellets or beans
- All-purpose thread to match fabrics
- Powdered blush
- Cotton swab
- Large-eye embroidery needle
- Basic sewing supplies and tools

Instructions

Note: All fabrics are sewn right sides together and with 3/8" seams unless otherwise stated.

Step 1. Trace and cut pieces as directed on patterns. Make 2" cuts ¼" apart on short ends of yellow felt for fringe. Cut ribbed section away from foot section of sock.

Step 2. Stitch head/body units together leaving opening for turning. Stitch arms together leaving end open for turning. Clip curves as indicated on patterns and trim corners diagonally.

Step 3. Turn arms and head/body unit right side out. Tightly stuff lower third of arms, head and upper 1" of body with polyester fiberfill. Place pellets or beans in body, then another layer of polyester fiberfill to fill body firmly. Slipstitch opening on body closed. Gather tops of arms with a running stitch and doubled, knotted thread. Pull up tightly and knot off securely.

Step 4. Sew feet together, leaving openings at top. Clip curves and turn right side out. Stuff firmly with polyester fiberfill to within 2½" of top. Turn top raw edges in and slipstitch legs to base of body with toes pointed inward.

Step 5. Sew inner and side seams of pants together. Turn and stitch a ¼" hem at leg bottoms and along top waist edges. Make a gathering stitch at the top of the pants, but do not pull or knot threads yet.

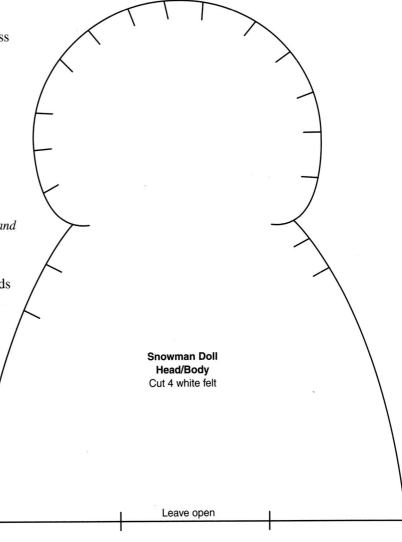

Snowman Doll
Head/Body
Cut 4 white felt

Leave open

Step 6. Place pants on body, pulling waist up to neck area. Pull gathering threads up tightly and knot.

Step 7. Place ribbed section of sock on the doll with the finished edge down. Fold up the bottom inch. Tuck the top of the sock to the inside.

Step 8. Slipstitch tops of arms to sides of doll just above the top of the sock sweater.

Step 9. Make a small stitch at center back of head, push needle through to center front, thread an eye button and push needle back through head and take a small stitch. Repeat for second eye, placing buttons side by side. Stitch red nose button just under eyes.

Step 10. Roll open edge of remaining sock section back twice to form a cuff. Pull sock over head so cuff touches the sweater at the sides. Slipstitch hat cuff to sweater. Make a gathering stitch around the top inch of the hat and pull up tightly.

Step 11. With embroidery floss, sew one novelty button to front of sweater and one to front cuff of hat. Stitch blue button to the top of the hat over the gathering stitch line.

Step 12. With a cotton swab, apply powdered blush to cheeks. Tie felt scarf around neck with a knot.

—*By Barbara Matthiessen*

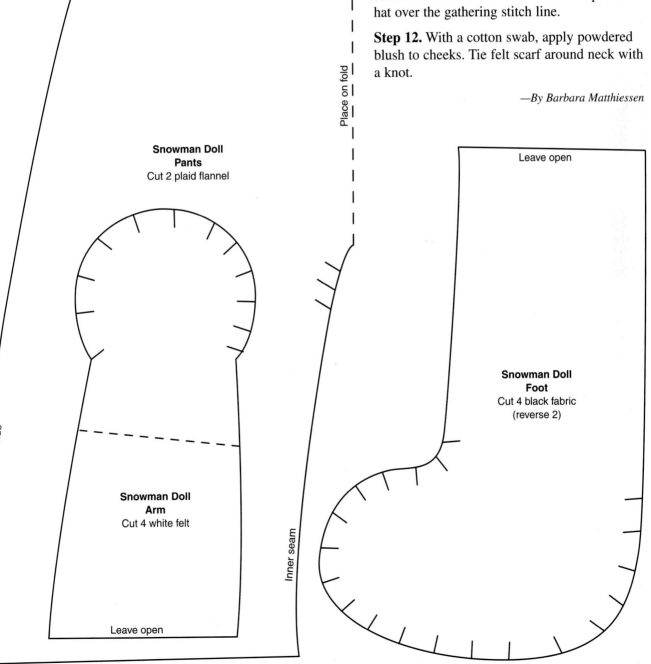

Top

Place on fold

**Snowman Doll
Pants**
Cut 2 plaid flannel

side

**Snowman Doll
Arm**
Cut 4 white felt

Inner seam

Leave open

Leave open

**Snowman Doll
Foot**
Cut 4 black fabric
(reverse 2)

Pincushion Doll

*A pincushion bustle at the back of her pretty floral-print apron makes
this little lady quite useful as she fits right into place in the sewing room.*

Project Specifications

Skill Level: Beginner

Doll Size: Approximately 16"

Materials

- 1 plastic 2-liter soda bottle
- ¼ yard white felt
- ⅔ yard pastel floral-on-white fabric
- ½ yard mauve-and-white stripe fabric
- ½ yard (½"-wide) white ruffled eyelet lace
- 1 (6") burgundy heart-shaped Battenburg lace doily
- 2 yards (⅝"-wide) rose ribbon
- Brown tightly curled hair
- 1 (2") wooden ball
- 1 (3½"-diameter) firm plastic-foam ball
- 6" gold 28-gauge wire
- Gold sewing scissors
- Polyester fiberfill
- 2 cups plastic pellets
- Skin-tone and rose acrylic paint
- Black fine-point permanent marker
- All-purpose thread to match fabrics
- Cotton swab
- Glue gun or tacky glue
- Serrated knife
- Air-drying disappearing marker
- Basic sewing supplies and tools

Instructions

Note: Use ¼" seam allowance unless otherwise noted.

Step 1. Pour plastic pellets into bottle. Glue around inside of bottle cap and replace.

Step 2. Cut two pieces 8¼" x 13" from white felt. Round off corners on one edge of each piece as shown in Fig. 1. Pin felt together and sew both long side seams, leaving open at top and 3" along center bottom. Turn right side out. Run a basting stitch along both openings. Pull 3" opening gathers tight and knot. Slip bottle inside. Pull remaining gathers tight around neck of bottle and knot threads.

Step 3. Paint the wooden ball with skin-tone acrylic paint. When dry, draw eyes, eyelashes and nose with permanent marker, referring to photo for placement. Apply blush to cheeks with cotton swab and rose acrylic paint. When dry, glue head to top of bottle cap.

Step 4. From mauve-and-white stripe fabric cut one piece 12½" x 42½" for petticoat. Sew short edges together. Turn right side out. For hem, fold under one raw edge ¼"; press. Turn under again, press and stitch. Run a basting stitch along other raw edge. Place dress over bottle and pull gathers tight under neck of bottle. Knot threads and spot with glue to secure.

Step 5. From pastel floral fabric cut one 12¼" x 42½" piece for dress. Sew short ends together and turn right side out. Fold under one raw edge ¼"; press. Turn under again, press and stitch. Run a basting stitch along raw edge, place dress over petticoat and pull gathers tight under head. Knot threads and spot with glue.

Step 6. Cut a 5" x 15" piece of floral fabric for arms. Fold piece in half lengthwise and stitch. Turn right side out and run a basting stitch across arm center. Pull gathers tight and knot. Lightly stuff each arm (either side of gathers). Overlap raw edges of both arms and run a basting stitch through all layers. Pull gathers tight and knot. Place arms over head and glue ends to back of dress.

Step 7. Cut a slit in heart-shaped doily from point to center. Cut a 1" circle at center as shown in Fig. 2. Place collar around neck with slit in back. Spot with glue to hold.

Fig. 2

Step 8. Wrap a strand of hair loosely around four fingers 10 times. Twist in center and glue to top of head. Continue gluing hair to head, filling in sides and back. Clip any loose strands and spot with glue to hold.

Step 9. Cut three 9" circles from pastel floral fabric. Right sides facing, sew two circles together around outer edge. Carefully cut a 2" slit in center of one circle and turn right side out; press. Run a basting stitch around circle 1" from outer edge. Pull up gathers slightly, add some stuffing and fit to top of head. Add more stuffing and adjust gathers if needed. Knot threads and glue bonnet to top of head.

Continued on page 108

Caterpillar Toy

Bright colors and soft maneuverable body parts make this an ideal toy for a toddler.
Pack the pieces in the diaper bag or keep them in the car for take-along fun.

Project Specifications

Skill Level: Beginner

Caterpillar Toy Size: Approximately 36" x 6"

Materials

- ½ yard red print
- ¼ yard dark red print
- ¼ yard black felt
- 9" x 18" pieces of yellow, blue, green, orange and purple print
- 9" x 18" pieces of yellow, blue, green, orange and purple solid
- 6 (1" x 1") hook-and-loop tape squares
- Polyester fiberfill
- All-purpose thread to match fabrics
- Heavy thread (rug, crochet or hand-quilting)
- 6-strand black embroidery floss
- 2 small jingle bells
- 2 (¾") wiggle-eye buttons
- Coiled wire bracelet
- Needle-nose pliers
- Craft glue
- Wooden spoon
- Basic sewing supplies and tools

Instructions

Step 1. Trace and cut head and face pieces as directed on pattern. Appliqué face on one head piece and embroider mouth with 3 strands of black embroidery floss. Sew eyes securely in place.

Step 2. Right sides together, sew head pieces together, leaving opening for turning. Turn right side out and stuff with polyester fiberfill, using wooden spoon to pack stuffing firmly and smoothly. Close opening.

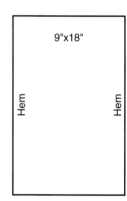

Fig. 1

Step 3. Cut one red print 9" x 18". Hem two long sides of 9" x 18" print piece as shown in Fig. 1. Fold in half with raw edges together, right sides facing, as shown in Fig. 2. Stitch with ½" seam allowance. Turn right side out.

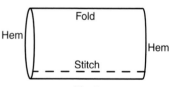

Fig. 2

Step 4. Work a zigzag stitch over heavy thread close to each

hemmed edge as shown in Fig. 3. Pull one end completely closed; tie to secure. Stuff firmly with polyester fiberfill. Pull up, close and secure remaining end. Secure knots with a drop of glue. Repeat steps 3 and 4 for each print fabric except dark red.

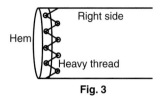

Fig. 3

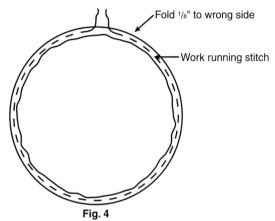

Fig. 4

Step 5. Cut two 8" circles from each solid fabric and from dark red print. Turn ⅛" under along raw edge. Work a running stitch with matching thread as shown in Fig. 4. Pull to gather as shown in Fig. 5. Flatten

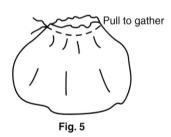

Fig. 5

puff for a yo-yo as shown in Fig. 6. Make two yo-yos each from five solid fabrics and dark red print.

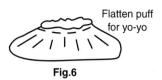

Fig.6

Step 6. Stitch one yo-yo on each side of coordinating print body segment, covering gathered sides of balls as shown in Fig. 7.

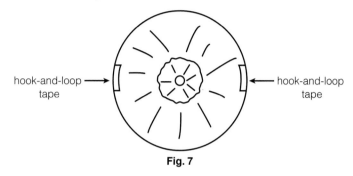

Fig. 7

Step 7. Stitch hook-and-loop tape squares between each body section.

Step 8. Cut feet as directed on pattern. Stitch on opposite sides of each body segment.

Step 9. Open wire bracelet; uncoil wires at one end with needle-nose pliers. Slip one jingle bell on each end of uncoiled wire. Twist wire ends to secure bells in place. Referring to photo, stitch in place on top of caterpillar's head for antennae.

—By Beth Wheeler

**Caterpillar Toy
Foot**
Cut 12 black felt

**Caterpillar Toy
Head**
Cut 2 red print
(adding 1/2" seam allowance)

**Caterpillar Toy
Face**
Cut 1 dark red print
(do not add seam allowances)

+ +

Enlarge 150% before cutting
for full-size pattern

Pin Cushion Doll

Continued from page 104

Step 10. Run a basting thread along outer edge of remaining circle. With serrated knife, cut foam ball in half and discard one half. Place ball, rounded side down, in center of fabric circle. Pull up gathers and knot threads. Adjust gathers evenly around edge of ball. Glue eyelet lace around outer inside edge of ball. Glue flat side of ball to back of dress, right below waist.

Step 11. Cut 12" piece of ⅜"-wide rose ribbon. Loop over center of arm, through scissors and tie a bow. Angle-cut ribbon ends. Cut 1 yard of rose ribbon and make a six-loop bow. Wrap center with wire and twist to secure. Cut off excess wire. Angle-cut ribbon ends. Glue to top of pincushion. Tie two small bows and angle-cut ends. Glue one to top of bonnet and one to front of doily at neck.

—*By Veleta "Sam"
Stafney*

Annie Angel Doll

This primitive little angel doll with her gauze wings, pastel dress and vintage embroidered linen apron will comfort and watch over someone you love.

Project Specifications

Skill Level: Beginner
Doll Size: Approximately 14"

Materials

Note: To make tea-stained muslin, spritz brewed tea onto muslin and let dry.

- ¼ yard tea-stained muslin
- ½ yard peach-and-green print fabric for dress
- 1 (⅜") peach button
- 4" scrap of lace
- Old embroidered doily for apron or 15" x 7" piece of white muslin
- ¼ yard green decorator gauze for wings
- 3" scrap of string for hanging loop
- Polyester fiberfill
- 10" (¼"-wide) peach ribbon
- 10" (⅛"-wide) green ribbon
- Fine-tip permanent black marker
- Brown acrylic paint for shoes
- Powdered blush
- Cotton swab
- 3 sprigs tiny dried flowers
- All-purpose thread to match fabrics
- Basic sewing supplies and tools

Instructions

Note: Use ¼" seam allowance unless otherwise noted.

Step 1. Trace and cut body pieces and dress bodice as directed on pattern pieces. Cut two 8" x 10" pieces peach and green print for skirt. Cut one 8" x 20" piece decorator gauze for wings.

Step 2. Sew arm and leg pieces together, leaving tops open for stuffing. Sew body pieces together leaving bottom open. Clip curves, turn right side out. Stuff arms and legs to stuff line with polyester fiberfill. Stuff body tightly.

Step 3. Insert legs ¼" into body opening and stitch opening closed. Paint shoes on feet using brown acrylic paint. Turn in top of arms ¼" and stitch tops of arms to body in position marked by X.

Step 4. Run gathering stitch across 8" side of each skirt piece. Gather and stitch each piece to one bodice bottom. Place right sides of bodice/skirt units together. Stitch shoulder seam, then underarm seam and dress side seam. Clip under arm. Hem bottom of skirt turning up ¼" twice.

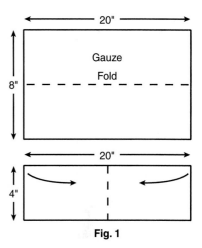

Fig. 1

Step 5. Fold decorator gauze in half and stitch around three sides leaving 2" opening for turning. Turn, stitch opening closed; press. Fold in 4" ends to center of gauze to form bow as shown in Fig. 1. Run a gathering stitch from bottom to top at center of gauze as shown in Fig. 2. Pull gathers up to make bow.

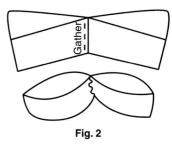

Fig. 2

Step 6. Gather 15" raw edge of doily or muslin; stitch to dress at skirt top to make apron.

Step 7. Place flower sprigs on top of each other forming a small bouquet. Tie to inside of hand using the green ribbon.

Step 8. Referring to pattern, draw Annie's face with fine tip permanent black marker. Blush cheek areas with cotton swab. Tie peach ribbon on head for hair. Stitch scrap of lace around neck and add button for collar.

Step 9. Stitch gathered decorator gauze onto back of Annie starting at back of neck and stitching tightly to center back. Make a loop for hanging at the back of neck from scrap of string.

—By Karen Mead

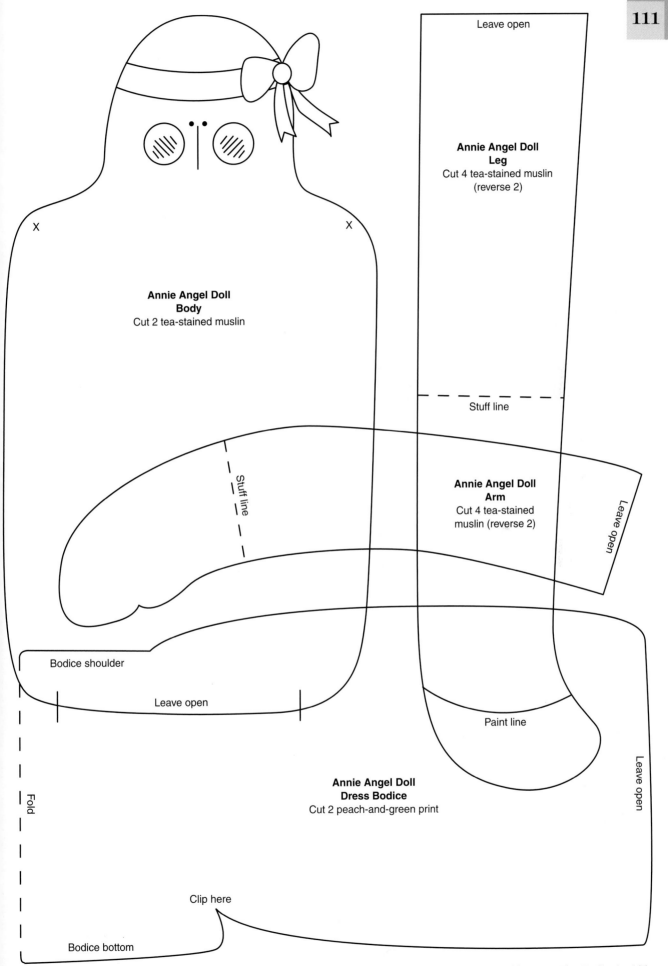

Leave open

**Annie Angel Doll
Leg**
Cut 4 tea-stained muslin
(reverse 2)

Stuff line

**Annie Angel Doll
Body**
Cut 2 tea-stained muslin

X   X

Stuff line

**Annie Angel Doll
Arm**
Cut 4 tea-stained
muslin (reverse 2)

Leave open

Bodice shoulder

Leave open

Paint line

Leave open

Fold

**Annie Angel Doll
Dress Bodice**
Cut 2 peach-and-green print

Clip here

Bodice bottom

Last-Minute Wearables

Young and young-at-heart enjoy compliments when wearing one-of-a-kind wearable art! Make a statement with whimsical appliqué, color-mixed fun wear, elegant crazy-patch, comfy denim, or easy-to-sew felt. From fun to fancy, wearables make great gifts for someone special—or as a treat for yourself!

Hair Scrunchies

Pigtails and ponytails will stay in place beautifully with these fun-to-make, frivolous hair accessories. Delight any little girl in your life!

Project Specifications

Skill Level: Beginner

Scrunchie Size: Approximately 5" diameter

Materials

- Variety of ribbons and rickrack (1 yard each, 3 or 4 colors)
- Variety of yarns (2 yards each, 4 or 5 colors)
- 8½" x 11" tagboard or card stock
- Package of ¼"-wide elastic
- Tape
- All-purpose thread to match trims
- Basic sewing supplies and tools

Instructions

Step 1. Cut tagboard in half lengthwise. Wrap ribbons, rickrack and yarns around the tagboard strip, taping ends to secure at edges of board. Wrap each with spaces between and fill in as layers and textures build. Do not layer more than your machine will be able to sew through.

Step 2. Sew a straight stitch down the center of the tagboard to secure all pieces together. With scissors, cut wrapped edges so loops no longer exist. The machine stitch will have perforated the tagboard. Carefully pull it apart and discard.

Step 3. Cut a 7" length of elastic. Place over previously sewn seam. Backstitch to secure and then zigzag down length of elastic, stretching elastic to its fullest. Stitch only a small section at a time, repositioning as you sew. When seam is complete, cut off excess elastic. Straight-stitch the two ends together, ribbons on the inside.

Step 4. Turn right side out. Shake and fluff with fingers. Should wrap one or two times around ponytail.

—By Kenna Prio

Fleecy Kitten Robe

Soft and cute as a newborn kitten. Pop this on any little girl after her bath and she'll purr when she snuggles up for her bedtime story.

Project Specifications

Skill Level: Beginner
Robe Size: All sizes

Materials

- Simplicity coat pattern 7822 (View D)
- Pink print fleece as directed on pattern for size
- 18" x 30" white chenille
- Scraps of pink felt
- ¼ yard fusible transfer web
- ¼ yard tear-away fabric stabilizer
- 1 yard (1"-wide) pink ribbon
- 4 (⅞") pink buttons
- 4 (¼") black buttons for eyes
- All-purpose thread to match fabrics
- White and pink rayon machine-embroidery thread
- Basic sewing supplies and tools

Instructions

Step 1. Follow pattern directions to make long coat using pink print fleece for robe and white chenille for collar and cuff trim.

Step 2. Trace kitten appliqué shapes (except body) onto paper side of fusible transfer web; cut out leaving roughly ½" margin around shapes.

Step 3. Fuse to wrong side of chenille and felt according to manufacturer's directions; cut out on tracing lines.

Step 4. Referring to photo for position, fuse kitten head and face parts to front of robe. Pin fabric stabilizer to wrong side of fleece behind appliqué area. Satin-stitch around appliqués using matching threads.

Step 5. Cut two kitten bodies from chenille. Fold top hem over twice and stitch. Pin body below head, overlapping slightly. Fuse tail to bottom of body.

Step 6. Place stabilizer behind body area. Satin-stitch around body and tail with matching threads leaving top open to form pocket.

Step 7. Make two bows from pink ribbon. Sew to top

of body, making sure to keep pocket open. Sew black button eyes in place.

—By Leslie Hartsock

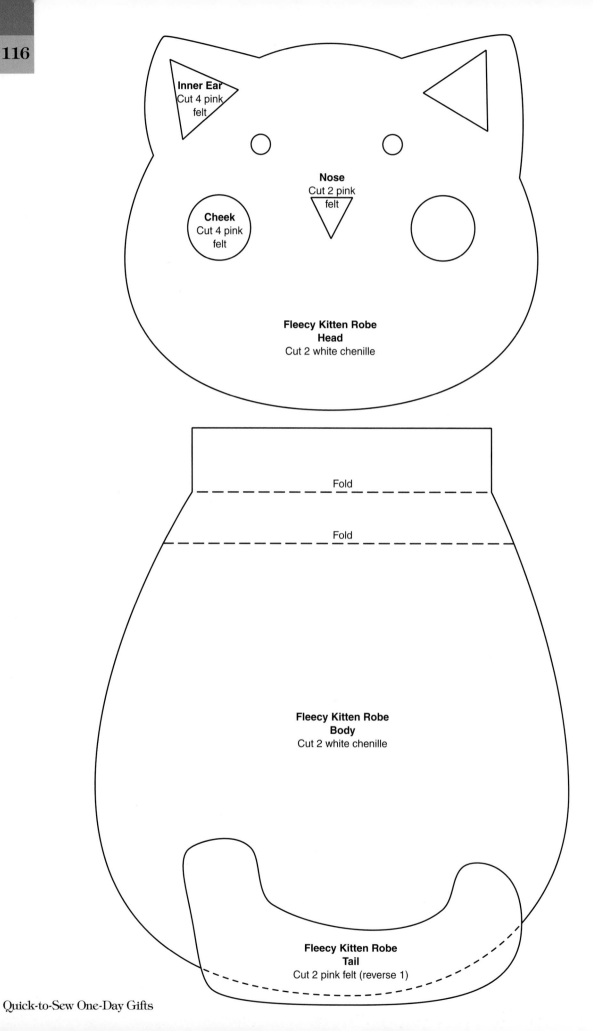

Inner Ear
Cut 4 pink
felt

Nose
Cut 2 pink
felt

Cheek
Cut 4 pink
felt

**Fleecy Kitten Robe
Head**
Cut 2 white chenille

Fold

Fold

**Fleecy Kitten Robe
Body**
Cut 2 white chenille

**Fleecy Kitten Robe
Tail**
Cut 2 pink felt (reverse 1)

Velvet Bag

This bag is big enough to be practical and pretty enough to be noticed.
Slip the trim little cord over your shoulder and wear it as an accessory to your dress.

Project Specifications

Skill Level: Beginner
Bag Size: Approximately 6½" x 8"

Materials

- ¼ yard each of two coordinating velvets
- ¼ yard satin for lining
- 1½ yards braid or cord for strap
- ⅔ yard (⅛"-wide) ribbon

- 3½" tassel
- Fancy button or brooch
- Basic sewing supplies and tools

Instructions

Step 1. Cut fabric pieces as directed on patterns.

Step 2. Right sides together, using ½" seam allowance, sew linings to velvet pieces, leaving a 3" opening at bottoms to turn. Snip corners and clip curves; turn

right side out. Slipstitch openings to close.

Step 3. Mark centers of each piece with pin near bottom edge.

Step 4. Cut ribbon in four equal pieces. Place two pieces along bottom edges of bag front lining and two along back lining. Stitch to each side to secure. Zigzag over ribbon to form casing as shown in Fig. 1, taking care not to catch ribbon in stitching. End stitching just short of center mark.

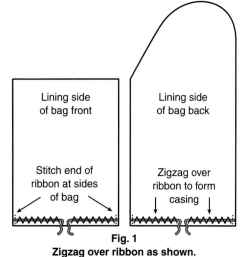

Fig. 1
Zigzag over ribbon as shown.

Step 5. With lining sides together, top-stitch bag front to bag back along sides ¼" from edges. Turn inside out.

Step 6. Pull drawstrings at the bottom tightly to gather; knot to hold. From right side insert tassel loop into center of gathers and stitch to hold.

Step 7. Turn bag right side out and hand-stitch the gathered bottom edges together, pulling the edges in as tightly as possible.

Step 8. Make a small opening near the top of the bag in each side seam. Insert end of strap braid into openings and knot inside the bag. Stitch back over seams to secure.

Step 9. Attach fancy button or brooch to flap.

—By Cindy Gorder

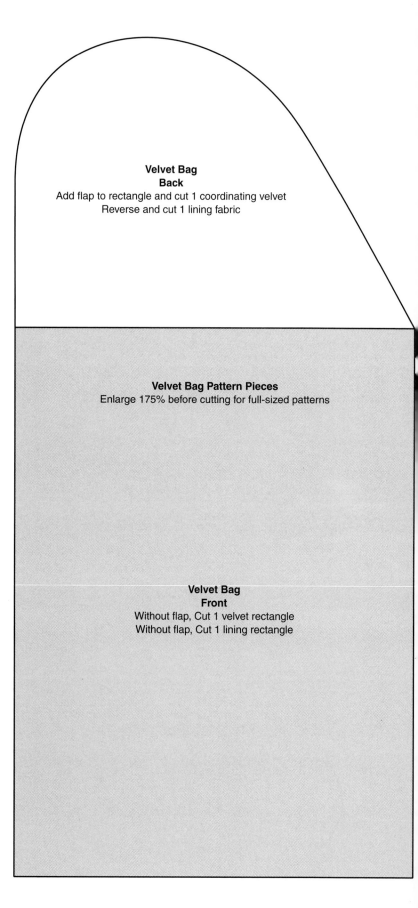

Velvet Bag
Back
Add flap to rectangle and cut 1 coordinating velvet
Reverse and cut 1 lining fabric

Velvet Bag Pattern Pieces
Enlarge 175% before cutting for full-sized patterns

Velvet Bag
Front
Without flap, Cut 1 velvet rectangle
Without flap, Cut 1 lining rectangle

Cabbage Rose Tote Bag

You'll love the wonderful effects you can achieve with brush-tip fabric markers.
You can complete this smart-looking carryall in less than an hour!

Project Specifications

Skill Level: Beginner

Tote Bag Size: Approximately 15" x 13" x 4"

Materials

- 2 pieces off-white canvas 18" x 20"
- Off-white and burgundy all-purpose sewing thread
- Fabrico brush-tip fabric markers from Tsukineko: #14 poppy red, #61 burgundy, #15 cherry pink, #33 rose pink, #40 mint and #60 celadon
- 60" (1"-wide) off-white canvas webbing
- Disappearing (air-drying) marker
- Basic sewing supplies and tools

Instructions

Step 1. Tape enlarged cabbage rose pattern to window or light box. Trace onto one piece of canvas with disappearing marker.

Step 2. With brush-tip markers and referring to photo, paint petals and bud with a blend of cherry pink and rose pink. Blend touches of burgundy along edges and add poppy red lines where indicated on pattern. Paint leaves, around bud and decorative wedges with mint. Blend celadon accents at the edges.

Step 3. Heat-set according to paint manufacturer's directions.

Step 4. Referring to photo, machine-stitch decorative lines and swirls around rose and extending to sides and bottom of bag. For the model, we used a chunky running stitch with off-white thread in the needle and burgundy thread in the bobbin.

Step 5. Cut bottom corners from two canvas pieces as shown in Fig. 1. With right sides of canvas facing,

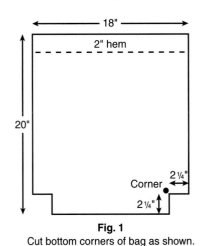

Fig. 1
Cut bottom corners of bag as shown.

18"

2" hem

20"

Corner

2¼"

2¼"

stitch side and bottom seams with ½" seam allowance. Press seams open.

Step 6. Match side and bottom seams to create bottom of tote and stitch as shown in Fig. 2.

Step 7. Turn under ¼" at top edge; press. Turn under 2" and stitch top hem.

Step 8. Cut off-white canvas webbing in half for two

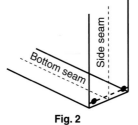

Bottom seam

Side seam

Fig. 2
Stitch bottom of bag as shown.

straps. Pin ends in position on bag front and back, extending 2½" into top of bag. Sew securely in place as shown in Fig. 3.

—By Judi Kauffman

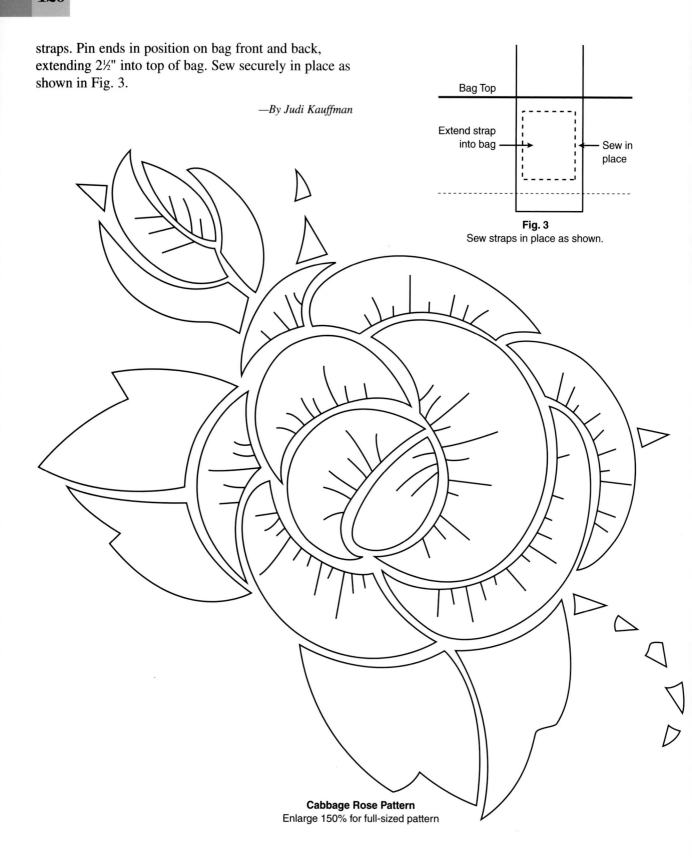

Bag Top

Extend strap into bag →

← Sew in place

Fig. 3
Sew straps in place as shown.

Cabbage Rose Pattern
Enlarge 150% for full-sized pattern

Memory Tote

Gather together an old photo, some buttons and trinkets of special significance and the pleasure of memorabilia will touch the recipient of this tote.

Project Specifications

Skill Level: Beginner

Tote Size: Approximately 12" x 14" x 2½"

Materials

- ⅔ yard tan canvas
- Zippered plastic bag
- ½ yard 2"-wide flat lace
- ⅔ yard ⅝"-wide lace with ribbon insert
- Assorted scraps of coordinating print fabrics and muslin
- 4" heart doily
- 10" round doily
- Assorted buttons and trinkets
- 4" x 5" photo
- Batting scrap

- Green 6-strand embroidery floss
- ⅓ yard (⅜"-wide) ribbon
- Ribbon rose
- Green pearl cotton
- Disappearing (air-drying) marker
- All-purpose thread to match fabrics
- Basic sewing supplies and tools

Instructions

Step 1. Cut two pieces tan canvas 15" x 18" and two strips 3½" x 24". Cut small and large pockets as directed on pattern.

Step 2. With right sides of each together, stitch around large and small pockets using ¼" seam allowance, leaving opening for turning. Clip curve and turn. Press piece flat, folding opening in. Press folds. Add buttons to flaps.

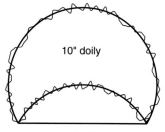

10" doily

Fig. 1
Fold 2½" of doily up and press.

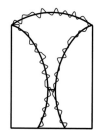

Fig. 2
Fold sides in and press.

Step 3. Fold 10" doily as shown in Fig. 1–3. Press each fold and baste to hold in place.

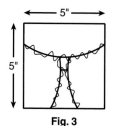

Fig. 3
Fold top flap down and baste.

Step 4. Cut a 4" x 5" piece from corner of plastic bag as shown in Fig. 4. Starting on the cut 4" side, place lace with ribbon insert on double plastic and stitch in place along both edges of ribbon. Stitch one 4" side only. Other three sides will be stitched when placed on tote.

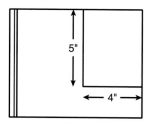

Fig. 4
Cut 4"x 5" corner from plastic bag.

Step 5. Cut heart pieces as directed on pattern. Place muslin pieces together and top with batting heart. Stitch around heart leaving opening for turning. Clip curves, turn heart and slipstitch opening closed. Stitch ribbon rose to heart.

Step 6. Cut two circles 3¼" in diameter, two circles 2½" and one circle 2" from print fabrics to make yo-yos. With wrong side of each circle facing you, fold over ¼" and stitch near edge around the outside of circle. Pull thread tight to form a closed circle, tucking in raw edges. Tie off tightly.

Step 7. Stitch 2"-wide lace in place 3" from right side of tote front. Place pockets and doily on tote front, referring to photo for placement. With disappearing marker, mark around each item. Use marks to guide stitching items in place, starting with heart doily, then three pockets and photo pocket.

Step 8. Fold each handle strip in half lengthwise. Stitch with ¼" seam allowance. Turn and press.

Step 9. With right sides of bag together, stitch around sides and bottom. Finish with pinking shears or serger. Stitch across corners of bag as shown in Fig. 5 to form gusset. Clip corners and turn right side out.

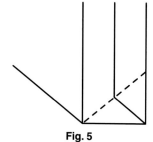

Fig. 5
Stitch across corners of bag to make gusset.

Step 10. Turn under ¼" at top of tote; press. Turn under another 2" and pin in place. Place handles 3" from each side seam, tucking raw edge under hem. Stitch hem; press handles up and stitch in place along top of bag.

Step 11. Stitch vine design along top front of bag using 2 strands of green embroidery floss. Attach yo-yos along vine as flowers. Trim bag with other charms, buttons and the stuffed heart. Add a special photo to the photo pocket.

—*By Karen Mead*

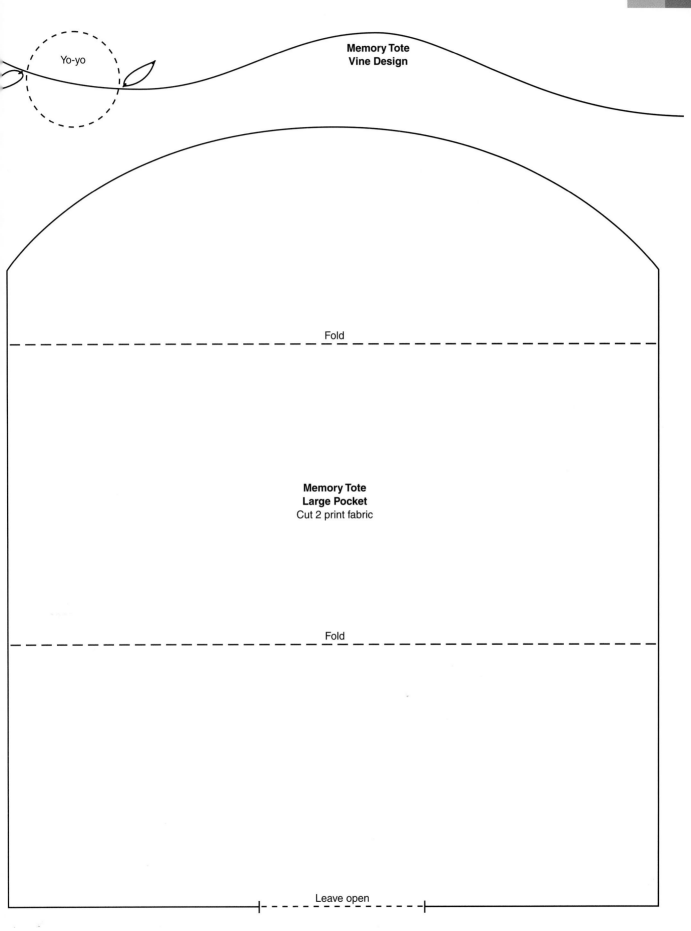

Yo-yo

**Memory Tote
Vine Design**

Fold

**Memory Tote
Large Pocket**
Cut 2 print fabric

Fold

Leave open

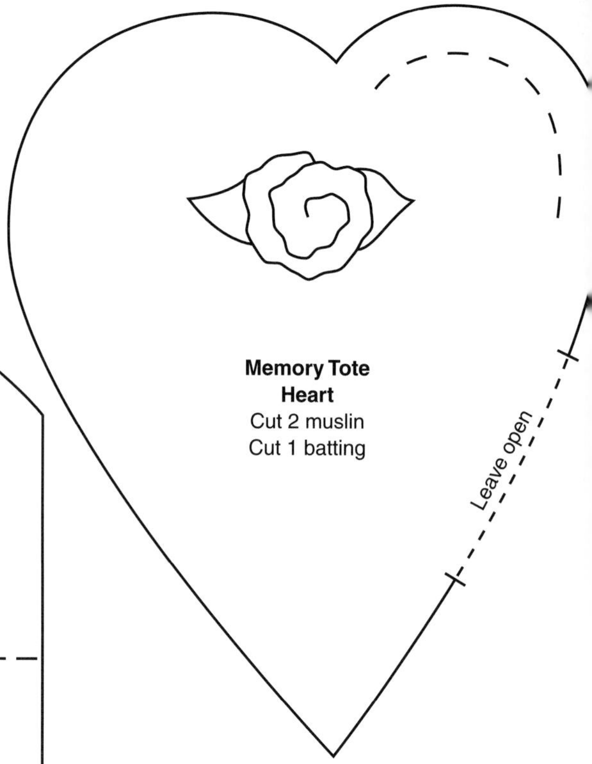

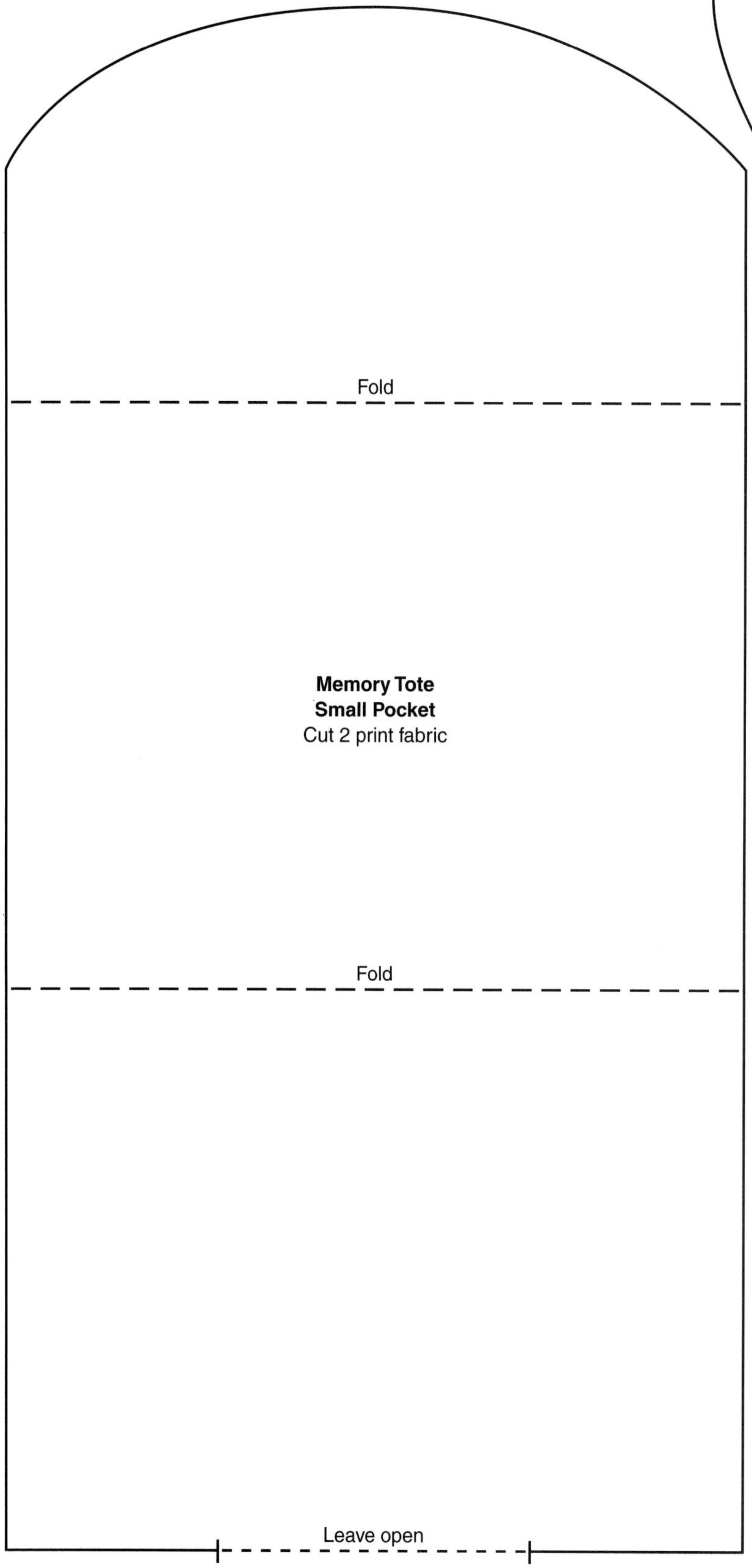

Fold

**Memory Tote
Small Pocket**
Cut 2 print fabric

Fold

Leave open

**Memory Tote
Heart**
Cut 2 muslin
Cut 1 batting

Leave open

Snowman Bag & Mittens

When there are flakes in the air, big kids and little kids think, "Snowman!" Make and give this white, fluffy set to your kids of any size so snowman can be anytime.

Project Specifications

Skill Level: Beginner
Bag Size: Approximately 12" x 14"
Mitten Size: All sizes

Materials

For Mittens

Note: Materials listed are for adult mittens. Reduce size of ribbing and bow fabric and size of buttons, snaps and felt circles proportionately for smaller mitten sizes.

- ¼ yard white plush felt
- ¼ yard white flannel
- 6" blue ribbing
- 2" x 42" torn fabric strip for bows
- 2 (¾") red shank buttons for noses
- 4 (8mm) black shank buttons for eyes
- 10 (2/0) black snaps for mouths

For Bag

- 12" x 28" white plush felt
- 2 pieces white flannel 12" x 14"
- 3¼" x 33" torn fabric strip for bow
- 1 (⅞") red shank button for nose
- 2 (⅝") black shank buttons for eyes
- 7 (1/0) black snaps for mouth
- 1 (1/0) silver snap for closure
- 43" blue 10 mm cording for handle
- 2 tassels to match cording
- 6-strand embroidery floss to match cording and tassels

For Mittens and Bag

- Scraps of pink felt
- Pink pearl cotton or 6-strand embroidery floss
- Black and white all-purpose thread
- Basic sewing supplies and tools

Instructions

Mittens

Note: Use ⅜" seam allowance unless otherwise noted.

Step 1. Trace around hand to establish pattern. Add 1" all around traced line for seam allowances.

Step 2. Cut 2 mitten shapes each from white felt and white flannel. Reverse pattern and repeat.

Step 3. Cut circles for cheeks as directed on pattern. Referring to photo, pin to mitten fronts of opposite hands. With pink pearl cotton or 2 strands of embroidery floss, buttonhole-stitch in place.

Step 4. Referring to photo, sew eye and nose buttons in place with white thread. Separate snaps and use only flatter side for mouth. Stitch in place with black thread.

Step 5. Right sides facing, sew felt mitten fronts and backs together. Trim close to seams to reduce bulk. Turn right side out.

Step 6. Sew flannel mitten liner fronts and backs together with ½" seam allowance. For extra strength, zigzag edges of the flannel liners. Clip almost to stitching line where thumb meets mitten. Do not turn right side out.

Step 7. Slip liners into mittens, matching thumbs and tips of hands. Pin to hold in place while adding ribbing.

Step 8. Measure one side of cuff edge of mitten. Multiply times 2 and subtract 1". Cut two pieces of 6" ribbing by this measurement. Sew short sides together to make ring. Fold ring in half lengthwise with seam to inside. Place one pin at the seam and another across from it as shown in Fig. 1.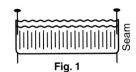

Fig. 1

Step 9. Pin raw edges of ribbing to raw edges of mitten, placing ribbing seam just to one side of mitten thumbside seam. Place other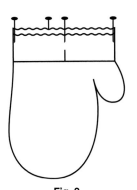

Fig. 2
Stitch ribbing around mitten as shown.

ribbing pin at other mitten side seam. Stretch ribbing as needed to fit around mitten as shown in Fig. 2. Straight-stitch ribbing to mitten. Remove pins and zigzag over mitten and ribbing seam.

Step 10. Cut torn fabric strip in half. Tie each half in a bow and tack center to a mitten.

Bag

Step 1. Fold white plush felt piece in half lengthwise, right sides together. Sew 14" sides together. Turn right side out.

Step 2. Cut circles for cheeks as directed on pattern. Pin circles to bag front using photo as placement guide. With pink pearl cotton or 2 strands of embroidery floss, buttonhole-stitch in place.

Step 3. Complete face as in Mittens Step 4.

Step 4. Stitch 14" sides of flannel liner together. Slide liner over the felt bag so right sides are together and top edges are even. Stitch around top of bag as shown in Fig. 3.

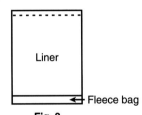

Fig. 3
Stitch around top of bag as shown.

Step 5. Pull liner up and away from bag. Stitch across open end (bottom) of liner. Trim seam to ⅛". Turn and press the cut edge toward the liner. Repeat the turn and press again, completely enclosing the raw edges of the liner. Topstitch close to last fold line as shown in Fig. 4.

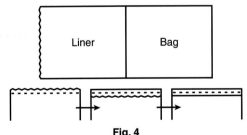

Fig. 4
Stitch across bottom of liner. Turn and press twice. Topstitch near last fold line.

Step 6. Push liner down inside bag. Topstitch along top edge of bag. Sew silver snap to center front and back of liner ¾" from top of bag.

Step 7. Stitch ends of cording with matching embroidery floss. Stitch into the center of the cord, wrap floss tightly around end and stitch back into the cord.

Step 8. Pin cording along side seams of bag with each wrapped end at a bottom corner. Slipstitch cord to sides of bag. Slipstitch tassels to end of cording with matching floss.

Step 9. Tie fabric strip in a bow. Tack center of bow to bag.

—By Barbara Matthiessen

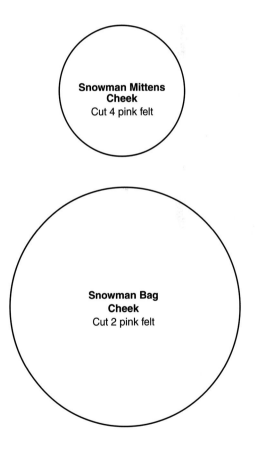

Snowman Mittens
Cheek
Cut 4 pink felt

Snowman Bag
Cheek
Cut 2 pink felt

Purse Accessories

Spend some pleasurable time with your children creating a special gift for teacher or grandmother. This project is easy enough for kids to enjoy success.

Project Specifications

Skill Level: Beginner
Card Holder Size: 2⅜" x 4¼"
Eyeglass Case Size: 3" x 6½"
Checkbook Cover Size: 7" x 3¾"

Materials

- 2 craft squares tan felt
- ¼ yard print lining fabric
- Scraps of tea-dyed muslin
- 6" x 7" lightweight bonding material
- 6-strand green and tan embroidery floss
- 5 (½") buttons
- Basic sewing supplies and tools

Note: To tea-dye muslin, soak scraps in brewed tea and let dry.

Instructions

Business Card Holder

Step 1. Cut pieces as directed on pattern. Center muslin piece on front felt piece with cutout and stitch in place with 1 strand tan embroidery floss. Stitch stem and leaf with 1 strand green embroidery floss. Add button for flower.

Step 2. With right sides of lining together, place front and back felt pieces on top and bottom facing outward and pin in place. With 2 strands of tan embroidery floss start stitching where indicated on pattern and work buttonhole stitch across back opening. At second stitching point stitch through all layers and continue around three sides of case, returning to starting point. Stitch through one felt and lining piece across front opening, knotting off at second stitching point.

Eyeglass Case

Step 1. Cut pieces as directed on pattern. Follow Business Card Holder Steps 1 and 2.

Checkbook Cover

Step 1. Cut pieces as directed on pattern. Stitch muslin as in Business Card Holder Step 1, adding three buttons as flowers.

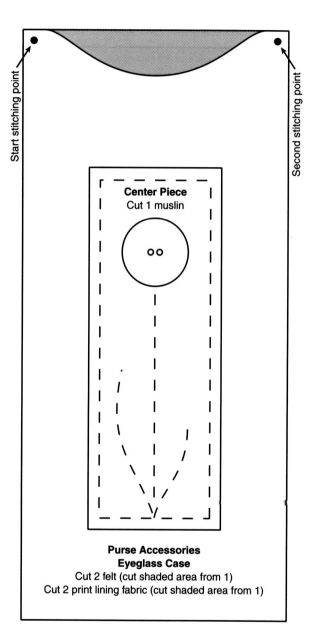

Purse Accessories
Eyeglass Case
Cut 2 felt (cut shaded area from 1)
Cut 2 print lining fabric (cut shaded area from 1)

Step 2. Cut two print fabric pieces 7" x 5" for pockets. Cut two pieces bonding material 7" x 3". Place one piece of bonding material on back of one pocket piece as shown in Fig. 1; fuse. Remove paper, fold pocket over top of bonding material and fuse as shown in Fig. 2. Repeat with other pieces.

Step 3. Place felt cover and lining wrong sides together. Place both pockets on top of lining as shown in Fig. 3. Pin in place.

Step 4. With buttonhole stitch and 2 strands of tan embroidery floss, stitch completely around periphery, stitching felt, lining and pockets together. Fold in half and insert checkbook.

—By Karen Mead

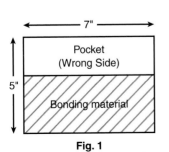

Fig. 1
Fuse bonding material to pocket as shown.

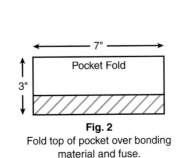

Fig. 2
Fold top of pocket over bonding material and fuse.

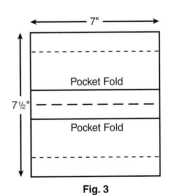

Fig. 3
Place wrong side of pockets over right side of checkbook lining as shown.

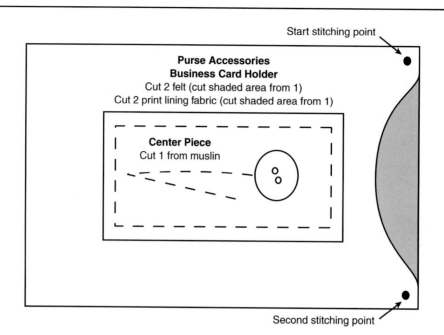

Center Fold Line

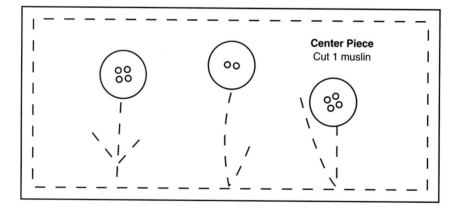

Halloween Shirt

*Scary bats, cats, ghosts and jack-o'-lanterns—put them all together
with your favorite denim and stitch up a boo-tiful shirt as a gift to yourself.*

Project Specifications

Skill Level: Beginner

Shirt Size: All sizes

Materials

- Long sleeve denim shirt
- Scraps of gold, yellow, black, orange and white fabric for appliqué
- Scraps of fusible transfer web
- Scraps of tear-away fabric stabilizer
- Rayon machine-embroidery thread to match appliqué pieces; pink, brown and green for details
- All-purpose thread to match fabrics
- 6 (¼") black beads
- 2 (⅝") wooden buttons
- 1 package yellow baby rickrack
- 6" (⅛"-wide) orange satin ribbon
- Basic sewing supplies

Instructions

Step 1. Prewash shirt and fabrics; do not use fabric softener.

Step 2. Trace appliqué shapes onto paper side of fusible transfer web; cut out leaving roughly ½" margin around shapes.

Step 3. Fuse to wrong side of selected fabrics according to manufacturer's directions; cut out on tracing lines.

Step 4. Topstitch baby rickrack down each side of front placket, around collar and cuffs.

Step 5. Position appliqué pieces, referring to photo. *Note: Appliqués are placed so two pockets may be used. If shirt has one or no pockets, position as desired.* Fuse in place.

Step 6. Pin tear-away fabric stabilizer on reverse of shirt behind each appliqué piece. Satin-stitch around each appliqué.

Step 7. Referring to pattern pieces, mark eyes on bat, eyes and mouth on ghosts and eyes, nose and whiskers on cat. Draw stem and curly vine on smallest pumpkin. Using a narrow satin-stitch, embroider details. Stitch bat and cat eyes and vine with green thread, ghost faces with black thread, cat whiskers with white thread and cat nose with pink thread. With brown

**Halloween Shirt
Small Pumpkin
Cut 1**

**Halloween Shirt
Ghost
Cut 3 white**

**Halloween Shirt
Cat
Cut 1 black**

**Halloween Shirt
Star
Cut 2 gold**

**Halloween Shirt
Bat
Cut 1 black**

thread, stitch stem on smallest pumpkin.

Step 8. Referring to photo, sew wooden buttons to stars and center black beads in ghost eyes.

Step 9. Tie a small bow with satin ribbon. Stitch to head of one ghost as shown in photo.

—By Michele Crawford

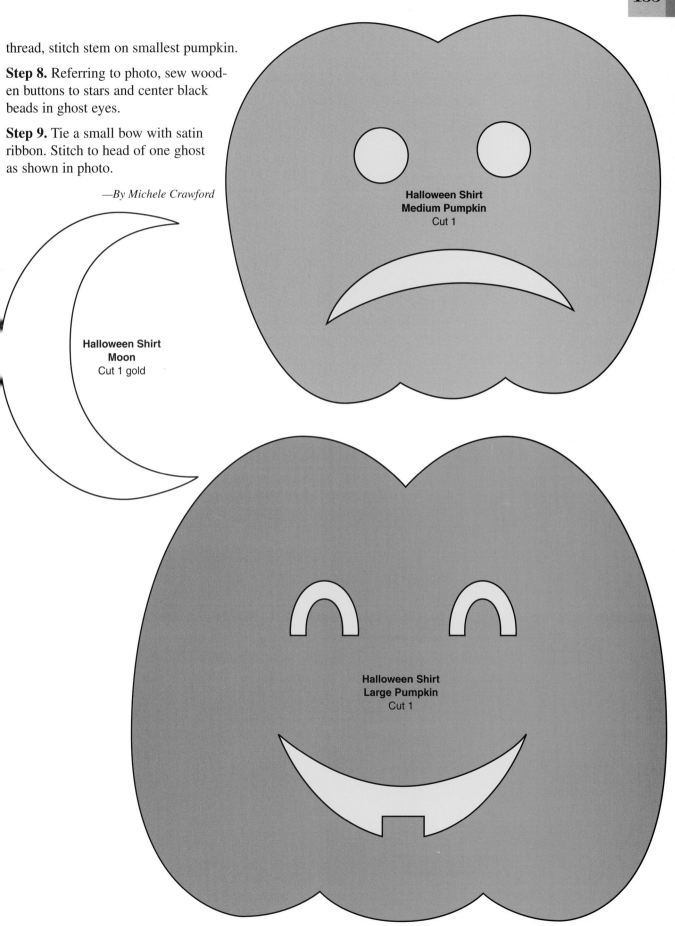

Halloween Shirt
Moon
Cut 1 gold

Halloween Shirt
Medium Pumpkin
Cut 1

Halloween Shirt
Large Pumpkin
Cut 1

Honeybee Cardigan

What could be more comfortable and appropriate than a garden sweatshirt embellished with busy bees and fresh daisies?

Project Specifications

Skill Level: Beginner

Cardigan Size: All sizes

Materials

- Sweatshirt in size of your choice
- Black, yellow, white and green scraps for appliqué
- ¾ yard accent fabric for binding and pockets
- Scraps of fusible transfer web
- Black 6-strand embroidery floss or black machine-embroidery thread
- All-purpose thread to match fabrics
- Basic sewing supplies and tools

Instructions

Step 1. Prewash sweatshirt and fabrics. Cut bottom, neck and sleeve ribbing off sweatshirt and cut sweatshirt up center front.

Step 2. Cut 3" bias strips and join to make 4 yards. Fold wrong sides together; press.

Step 3. Starting at center back, sew raw edges of binding all around right side of cut edges of jacket. Overlap ends at center back and cut off excess. Turn folded edge of bias to inside and slipstitch in place. Repeat on each sleeve.

Step 4. Cut pockets as directed on pattern. Place two pieces right sides together and sew around periphery with ¼" seam allowance, leaving a 2" opening in the top for turning. Clip seams and turn. Press opening to inside and topstitch across pocket top. Repeat for second pocket.

Step 5. Trace appliqué shapes onto paper side of fusible transfer web as directed on patterns; cut out leaving roughly ½" margin around shapes.

Step 6. Fuse to wrong side of selected fabrics according to manufacturer's directions; cut out on tracing line.

Large Flower Stem
Cut 1 green

Large Stripe
Cut 5 yellow
(reverse 3)

Small Stripe
Cut 5 yellow
(reverse 3)

**Honeybee Cardigan
Bee Body**
Cut 5 black (reverse 3)

**Honeybee Cardigan
Bee Wing**
Cut 10 white

**Honeybee Cardigan
Pocket**
Cut 4 accent fabric

**Honeybee Cardigan
Large Flower Leaf**
Cut 2 green

**Honeybee Cardigan
Large Flower Center**
Cut 1 yellow

Small Flower Stem
Cut 2 green (reverse 1)

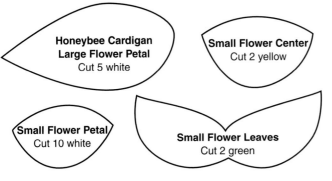

**Honeybee Cardigan
Large Flower Petal**
Cut 5 white

Small Flower Center
Cut 2 yellow

Small Flower Petal
Cut 10 white

Small Flower Leaves
Cut 2 green

Step 7. Position appliqué pieces, referring to photo. Fuse in place.

Step 8. Buttonhole-stitch around each appliqué by hand with 2 strands of black embroidery floss or by machine with black machine-embroidery thread.

Step 9. Referring to photo for placement, stitch the pockets in place.

—*By Pearl L. Krush*

Last-Minute Wearables

Chenille/Fleece Jacket

When it warms up enough to put away winter coats, unleash your creativity
and fashion a scrumptious fluffy jacket to ward off any chill in the air.

Project Specifications

Skill Level: Intermediate

Jacket Size: All sizes

Materials

- McCalls pattern 9524
- Cream fleece required by pattern
- ½ yard thin batting
- ½ yard cream cotton lining fabric
- White and cream chenille scraps in wide variety of textures
- 6 yards total of wide variety of cream and white trims
- All-purpose thread to match fabric
- Cream and white 6-strand embroidery floss
- Buttons, charms, beads, pearls and decorative appliqués for embellishment
- Basic sewing supplies and tools

Fold

Chenille/Fleece Jacket
Back Top Yoke
Cut 1 batting,
adding seam allowance

Enlarge by 134%

Instructions

Step 1. Using purchased pattern, cut fronts, back, front facings, sleeves and back middle yoke from cream fleece. Cut collar, cuffs and yokes as directed on patterns from batting for piecing foundations. Cut cuff and collar linings as purchased pattern instructs.

Extend as necessary

Step 2. Sew a variety of shapes, textures and shades of chenille to batting foundation pieces. Sew and flip pieces as shown in Fig. 1 to completely cover foundations. Sew ribbons and trims over each seam. Refer to photo for ideas.

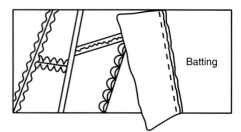

Fig. 1
Sew and flip chenille pieces to cover batting. Cover seams with trims.

Batting

Fold

**Chenille/Fleece Jacket
Back Bottom Yoke**
Cut 1 batting,
adding seam allowance

Extend as necessary

Step 3. Place yoke pieces over jacket fronts and back. Stay-stitch edges and cover edges with trim.

Step 4. Follow purchased pattern instructions for assembly, lining collar and cuffs.

Step 5. Embellish as desired. Hand-stitch buttons, charms, beads and pearls in place, striving for balance as you go. Add decorative appliqués with white and cream embroidery floss. Add trim around bottom of jacket.

—By Kenna Prior

**Chenille/Fleece Jacket
Middle Yoke**
Cut 1 fleece,
adding seam allowance
Cut 2 batting
without fold for front,
adding seam allowance

Extend as necessary

Child's Denim Coat

This basic coat pattern, sewn in popular denim and trimmed with soft, cuddly chenille, goes together quickly and easily and will go right to a little girl's heart.

Project Specifications

Skill Level: Intermediate

Coat Size: All sizes

Materials

- McCalls pattern 2403
- Blue denim as required by pattern
- ¼ yard thin batting
- ¼ yard lining fabric
- Wide variety of colors and textures of chenille scraps
- Total of 4 yards mixed ribbons and trims
- All-purpose thread to match fabrics
- 6-strand embroidery floss to match trims and chenille
- 4 (1⅛") self-covered buttons
- Variety of buttons, charms, beads, pearls and appliqués for embellishment
- Basic sewing supplies and tools

Instructions

Step 1. Using purchased pattern, cut fronts, back, sleeves and facings from denim. Cut collar and cuffs from batting for piecing foundations. Cut linings as directed on purchased pattern. Cut hearts as directed on pattern.

Step 2. Sew a variety of shapes, textures and shades of chenille to batting foundation pieces. Sew and flip pieces as shown in Fig. 1 to completely cover foundations. Sew ribbons and trims over each seam. Refer to

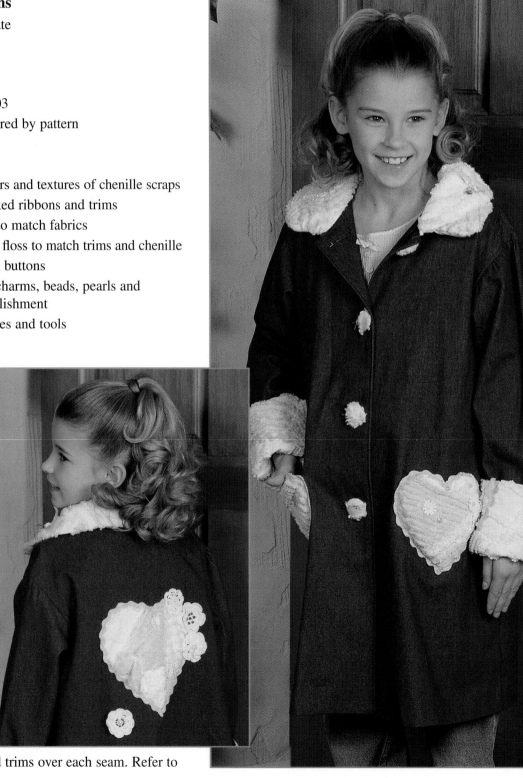

Fig. 1
Sew and flip chenille pieces to cover
batting. Cover seams with trims.

photo for ideas.

Step 3. Follow purchased pattern instructions for coat assembly, lining collar, cuffs and heart pockets. Topstitch large heart to center back of coat.

Step 4. Cover self-covered buttons with chenille. Work buttonholes on right front.

Step 5. Embellish as desired. Hand-stitch buttons, charms, beads and pearls in place, striving for balance as you go. Add decorative appliqués with embroidery floss.

—*By Kenna Prior*

Child's Denim Coat

Large Heart
Cut 1 batting

Small Heart
Cut 2 batting
Cut 2 lining

Beaded Amulet Bag

This eye-catching bag has a vintage quality that reflects a special place in time.
It has room for a few tiny treasures and offers an opportunity to try simple beading.

Project Specifications
Skill Level: Beginner
Amulet Bag Size: Approximately 1½" x 2½"

Materials
- 6"–8" of 1½"-wide patterned ribbon

Note: Size of pattern will determine length. Should be at least one complete pattern centered on front and back. Allow ¼" seam allowance on each end of ribbon. Printed fabric may be substituted for ribbon, but add ¼" side seam allowances.

- 1½"-wide ribbon for lining, ½" shorter than patterned ribbon
- Assortment of seed, rocaille, bugle and specialty beads in assorted sizes and colors
- Beading thread to match ribbon
- Beading, #20 embroidery or #9 milliner's needle
- Double-sided sticky tape
- Tweezers
- 1 yard cord, rattail, soutache braid or ribbon for ties
- Basic sewing supplies and tools

Instructions
Step 1. Sew, zigzag, serge or use a line of clear-drying glue to stabilize the cut ends of patterned and lining ribbons.

Step 2. Determine placement of beads to embellish patterned ribbon.

Step 3. Thread needle and knot thread. Backstitch several times on wrong side of patterned ribbon under location of first bead. Come up through ribbon, through bead from left to right and down through ribbon. Next to where needle went down, come back up through ribbon and back through same bead from right to left. Backstitch under bead to secure. Continue beading design in same manner until ribbon is completed as desired.

Step 4. Put right sides of beaded and plain ribbons together and sew each end. Turn right side out. Lining is shorter than patterned ribbon, so a portion of the front ribbon will be turned to the inside to form a smooth top edge.

Step 5. Starting at the open ends, machine-stitch side seams together. Stitch close to ribbon edge.

Step 6. Place three strips (one for each side and bottom of bag) double-sided sticky tape on a piece of white paper. With tweezers, place beads on each strip in desired color and shape arrangements. Each piece of fringe should be different from its neighbor but have a seed bead at the end. See Fig. 1 for arrangement ideas.

Note: Tape will hold beads in place while working but allow for changes.

Step 7. For each fringe section, attach a knotted length of thread in the seam inside the bag. Run threaded

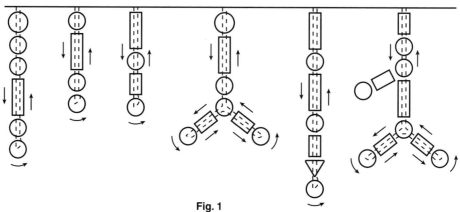

Fig. 1
Suggested bead placement for fringe.

needle through selected beads. Reinsert needle in the line of beads, but do not go through the final seed bead. Go back through beads to ribbon edge. Backstitch into ribbon edge to secure fringe section. Repeat for remaining fringe sections.

Step 8. A continuous strand of assorted beads long enough to fit over the head may be used for finishing.

For adjustable ties sew a length of cord, rattail, soutache braid or ribbon to each top corner of the amulet. Allow enough length to tie an adequate bow.

Step 9. Tie a knot at the free end of each cord to prevent fraying.

—By Donna Friebertshauser

Bright Fleece Jacket

Fleece is a wonderfully easy fabric to sew and it comes in a wide variety of colors. Enjoy mixing and matching hot colors for this playful cropped girl's jacket.

Project Specifications

Skill Level: Beginner

Jacket Size: All sizes

Materials

- Simplicity coat pattern 7822
- ½ yard less fuchsia fleece than suggested for length of coat
- ½ yard lime green fleece
- ⅙ yard yellow fleece
- ¼ yard purple fleece
- ½ yard orange fleece

Note: Suggested fabric amounts are for size BB (5, 6, 6X). For smaller or larger sizes, adjust accordingly.

- ½ yard fusible interfacing
- ⅛ yard yellow lining fabric
- All-purpose thread to match fabrics
- 4 (1") flower buttons
- Basic sewing supplies and tools

Instructions

Step 1. Cut one collar each from purple and yellow fleece.

Step 2. Cut two sleeves from lime green fleece. Omit facings and cuffs.

Step 3. Measure down 5" from pattern waistline mark and draw new length line for jacket body and front facing (if desired, shorten or lengthen for intended wearer).

Step 4. Cut back and right front from fuchsia fleece. Reverse pattern front and cut left front from orange fleece.

Step 5. Cut one back neck facing from purple fleece.

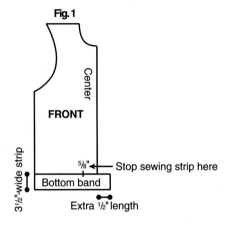

Fig. 1

Cut right front facing from fuchsia fleece. Reverse pattern and cut left front facing from orange fleece. Stitch facings and collar in place as directed on pattern.

Step 6. Measure bottom of jacket back. Cut a 3½" strip of purple fleece by that size. Right sides together, stitch strip to fuchsia jacket back.

Step 7. Measure bottom of jacket front and add ½". Cut two strips 3½" by that size. Right sides together, stitch strips to each jacket front, stopping ⅝" from jacket front edge.

Step 8. Measure bottom of sleeve. Cut two 3½" strips purple fleece of purple fleece by that size. Right sides together, stitch a strip to each sleeve.

Step 9. Sew sleeve and side seams. Turn raw edges of purple fleece trim to inside and slipstitch to seam.

Step 10. Topstitch ¼" from edge of collar and fronts of jacket using matching threads.

Step 11. Place and stitch buttons and buttonholes.

—By Leslie Hartsock

Patchwork Vest

Stitch this vest in jewel tones and lush fabrics and pair it with black velvet pants or a long, skinny skirt for a very dressy look.

Project Specifications

Skill Level: Beginner

Vest Size: All sizes

Materials

- Vest pattern of your choice
- ½ yard paisley-print corduroy
- ½ yard burgundy velour
- ½ yard green velour
- 1½ yards black lining fabric
- 3 yards (⅜"-wide) black grosgrain ribbon
- 1 yard lightweight fusible interfacing
- Tracing paper
- All-purpose thread to match fabrics
- Basic sewing supplies and tools

Instructions

Step 1. Trace two vest fronts each from tracing paper and interfacing. Reverse one interfacing piece.

Step 2. Mark patchwork pattern and grain line on each tracing paper front as shown in Fig. 1.

Step 3. Trace shapes onto fusible side of interfacing fronts.

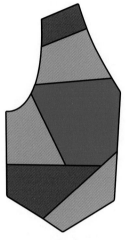
Fig. 1

Fig. 2

Step 4. Cut tracing paper pattern apart along drawn lines and pin to fabrics, matching grain lines. Cut out and place onto fusible side of interfacing. Press first from the fabric side and then from the interfacing side.

Step 5. Place grosgrain ribbon over seam lines and stitch in place as shown in Fig. 2.

Step 6. Finish vest according to pattern directions using black lining fabric for back and all linings.

—By Sandy Garrett

The Night Before the Christmas Gift Exchange

Tomorrow is that special party—the one you've been looking forward to for weeks. Gifts will be exchanged, revealing the identity of the secret pal you've guessed about all year. Too bad you haven't had time to make that elaborate gift planned months ago.

Not to worry! We've collected projects from designers across the nation—just to help you maintain a cheerful holiday spirit. Choose from tree skirts, stockings, ornaments, wall hangings, wearables and more. In just a few hours, the gift will be ready to wrap and you can relax by the fireplace with a cup of hot cocoa and a cookie. Happy holidays!

Holly Berry Christmas

*Call into action any member of your family who can wield a pair of scissors,
because anyone can join the fun of making this coordinated Christmas collection.*

Project Specifications

Skill Level: Beginner
Tree Skirt Size: Approximately 50" diameter
Banner Size: Approximately 26" x 10"
Ornament Size: Approximately 5" x 5"
Tree Topper Size: Approximately 9" x 7"

Materials

- 3¼ yards 36"-wide cream felt
- 1¼ yards 36"-wide red felt
- ½ yard 36"-wide green felt
- ¾ yards fusible transfer web
- 1½ yards gold string
- Polyester batting and fiberfill
- All-purpose thread to match felt
- 3 (½") O rings
- Basic sewing supplies and tools

Instructions

Tree Skirt

Step 1. Trace and cut patterns. Join panel pattern pieces on marked line.

Step 2. Trace and cut felt skirt pieces as directed on templates. Trace appliqué shapes onto paper side of fusible transfer web; cut out leaving roughly ½" margin around shapes.

Step 3. Place wrong side of panel trim on right side of panel, overlapping ½". Pin and sew in place with zigzag stitch. Repeat for 16 panels.

Step 4. Sew panels together with ¼" seam allowance, leaving one panel unsewn for opening. Press seams open.

Step 5. Fuse appliqué shapes to wrong side of felt according to manufacturer's directions; cut out on tracing lines.

Step 6. Referring to photo, position appliqué pieces; fuse in place. With matching threads, zigzag-stitch around each piece.

Step 7. Place the tree skirt collar over the center of the sewn panels, overlapping the skirt so that the open ends meet with the opening of the skirt. Pin and sew in place with a straight stitch. Topstitch ½" above the first stitching line.

Step 8. Cut tie 2½" x 36" from red felt. Fold tie in half lengthwise. Center and sandwich inner edge of collar between raw edges of tie. Zigzag-stitch entire length of raw edges to finish.

Tree Topper

Step 1. Trace patterns and cut felt pieces as directed on template. Trace appliqué pieces onto paper side of fusible transfer web; cut out leaving roughly ½" margin around shapes.

Step 2. Fuse appliqué pieces to wrong side of felt according to manufacturer's directions and cut out on tracing lines.

Step 3. Referring to photo, position appliqué pieces; fuse in place. With matching threads, zigzag- or buttonhole-stitch around each piece.

Step 4. Place front and back of star wrong sides together and stitch 1⁄4" from edge. Leave opening for stuffing.

Step 5. Stuff star firmly with fiberfill and finish stitching.

Step 6. Cut a 3" x 8" strip of felt for hanger. Fold long edges to center. Bring short edges together and overlap ends to form a ring. Sew ring to back of star and use to slip over the top of tree.

Ornaments

Step 1. Trace ornament patterns and cut felt and batting pieces as directed on templates.

Step 2. Trace and sew appliqué pieces as directed in Tree Topper, Steps 1–3

Step 3. Sandwich batting between front and back pieces. Cut gold string in 10" lengths. Knot ends together and slip knotted ends into top of each ornament. Topstitch 1⁄4" from outer edge of each ornament.

Welcome Banner

Step 1. Trace and cut out patterns; join on marked lines. Cut felt background pieces as directed on pattern.

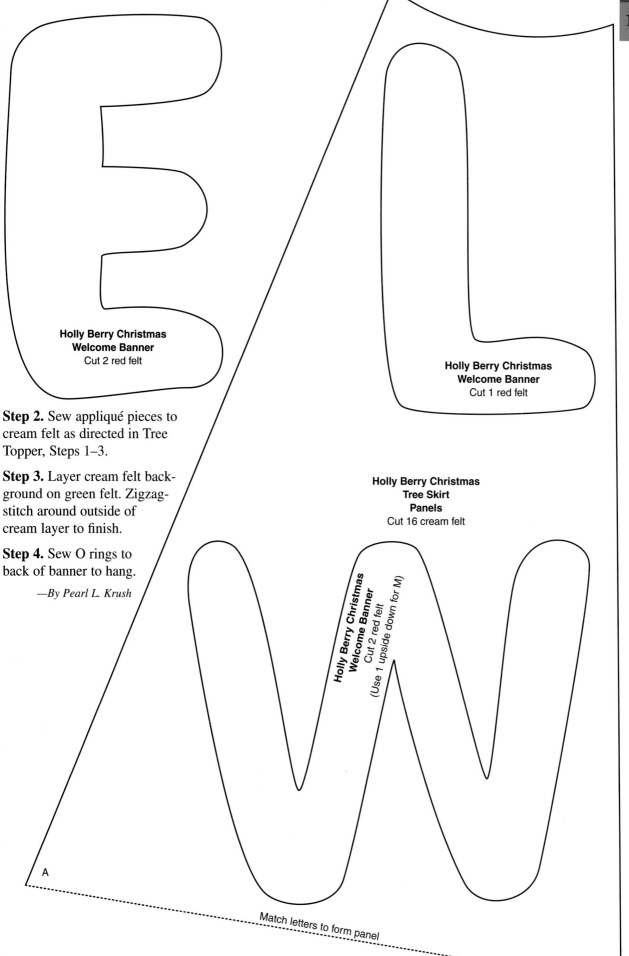

**Holly Berry Christmas
Welcome Banner**
Cut 2 red felt

**Holly Berry Christmas
Welcome Banner**
Cut 1 red felt

Step 2. Sew appliqué pieces to cream felt as directed in Tree Topper, Steps 1–3.

Step 3. Layer cream felt background on green felt. Zigzag-stitch around outside of cream layer to finish.

Step 4. Sew O rings to back of banner to hang.

—By Pearl L. Krush

**Holly Berry Christmas
Tree Skirt
Panels**
Cut 16 cream felt

**Holly Berry Christmas
Welcome Banner**
Cut 2 red felt
(Use 1 upside down for M)

A

B

Match letters to form panel

**Holly Berry Christmas
Welcome Banner**
Cut 1 red felt

**Holly Berry Christmas
Tree Skirt
Panel Trim**
Cut 16 red felt

Fold

**Holly Berry Christmas
Tree Skirt Collar**
Cut 16" x 16" red felt; fold twice
Place pattern on folds and cut

Enlarge Tree Skirt Collar pattern 125%

Fold

**Holly Berry Christmas
Welcome Banner**
Cut 1 red felt

**Holly Berry Christmas
Tree Skirt Panels**
Cut 16 cream felt

A

**Holly Berry Christmas
Welcome Banner**
Join paper pattern pieces before cutting felt.
Cut 1 cream felt
Cut 1 green felt 1" larger all around
Enlarge 112%

Match letters to form pattern

B

A

The Night Before Christmas Gift Exchange

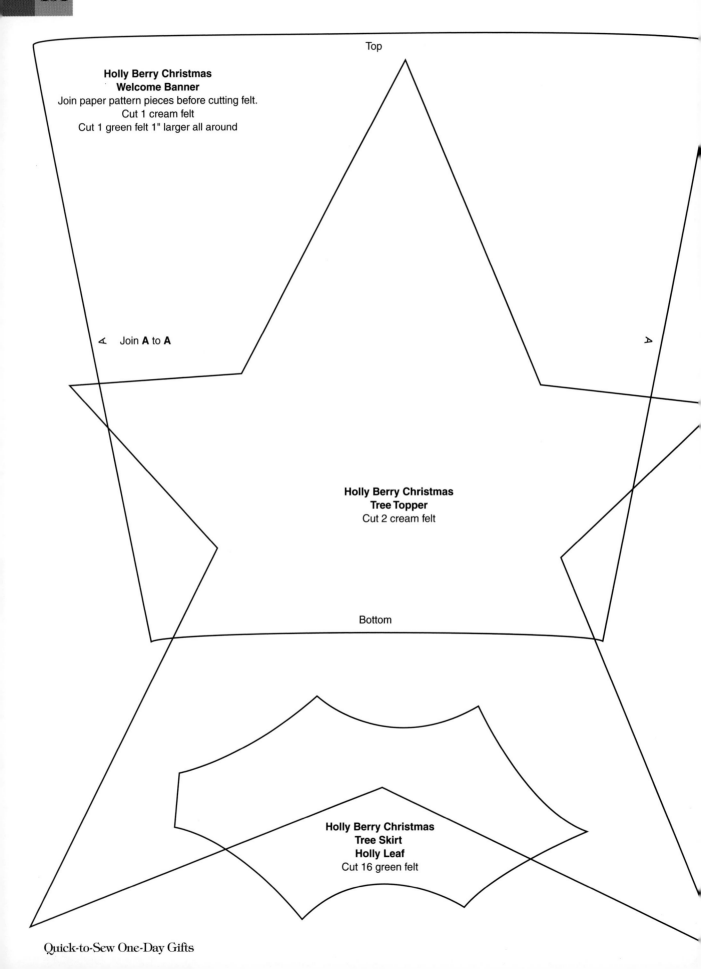

Top

**Holly Berry Christmas
Welcome Banner**
Join paper pattern pieces before cutting felt.
Cut 1 cream felt
Cut 1 green felt 1" larger all around

Join **A** to **A**

A

A

**Holly Berry Christmas
Tree Topper**
Cut 2 cream felt

Bottom

**Holly Berry Christmas
Tree Skirt
Holly Leaf**
Cut 16 green felt

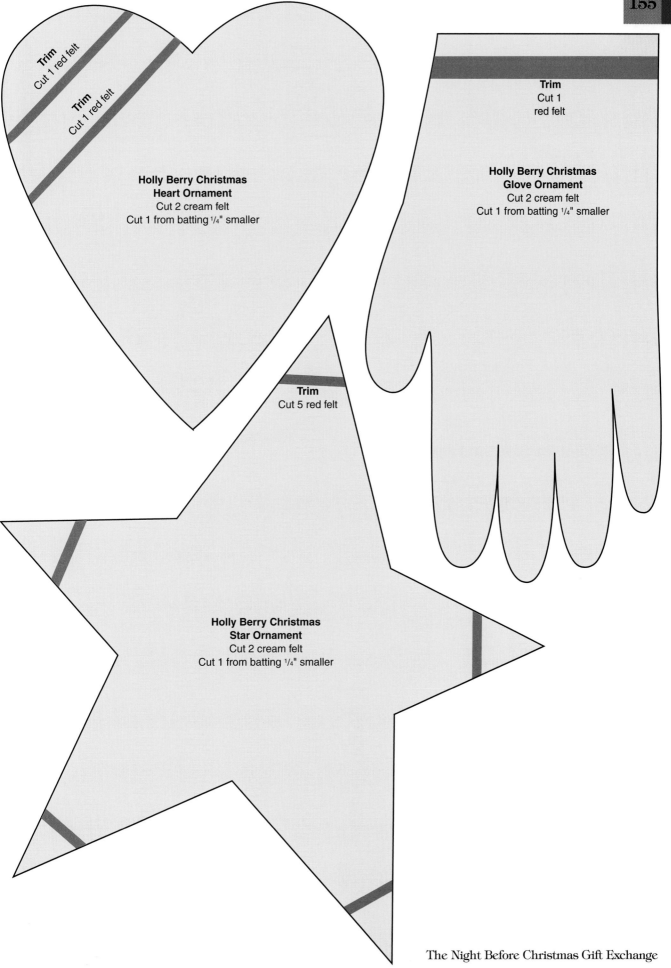

Trim
Cut 1 red felt

Trim
Cut 1 red felt

**Holly Berry Christmas
Heart Ornament**
Cut 2 cream felt
Cut 1 from batting 1/4" smaller

Trim
Cut 1
red felt

**Holly Berry Christmas
Glove Ornament**
Cut 2 cream felt
Cut 1 from batting 1/4" smaller

Trim
Cut 5 red felt

**Holly Berry Christmas
Star Ornament**
Cut 2 cream felt
Cut 1 from batting 1/4" smaller

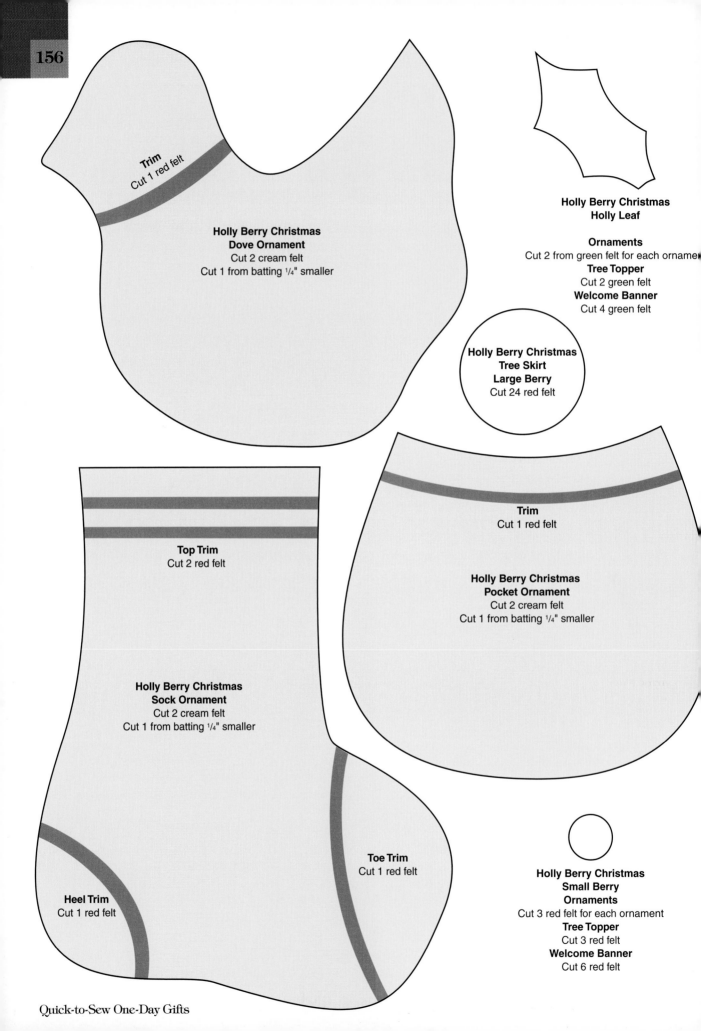

Trim
Cut 1 red felt

Holly Berry Christmas
Dove Ornament
Cut 2 cream felt
Cut 1 from batting ¼" smaller

Holly Berry Christmas
Holly Leaf

Ornaments
Cut 2 from green felt for each ornament
Tree Topper
Cut 2 green felt
Welcome Banner
Cut 4 green felt

Holly Berry Christmas
Tree Skirt
Large Berry
Cut 24 red felt

Trim
Cut 1 red felt

Holly Berry Christmas
Pocket Ornament
Cut 2 cream felt
Cut 1 from batting ¼" smaller

Top Trim
Cut 2 red felt

Holly Berry Christmas
Sock Ornament
Cut 2 cream felt
Cut 1 from batting ¼" smaller

Toe Trim
Cut 1 red felt

Heel Trim
Cut 1 red felt

Holly Berry Christmas
Small Berry
Ornaments
Cut 3 red felt for each ornament
Tree Topper
Cut 3 red felt
Welcome Banner
Cut 6 red felt

Angel Friends

Bless the homes of your special friends with a company of sweet angels.
The stocking is a perfect holder for homemade goodies or small specialty gifts.

Project Specifications

Skill Level: Beginner
Quilt Size: 10" x 13"
Stocking Size: Approximately 10" x 12"

Materials

- ⅓ yard blue fabric
- ⅓ yard muslin
- ⅛ yard gold fabric
- Red scraps for appliqué
- Scraps of fusible transfer web
- ⅓ yard fabric stabilizer
- All-purpose thread to match fabrics
- Rayon embroidery thread to match fabrics
- 1 spool white machine-quilting thread
- Thin batting 12" x 15"
- 1½ yards purchased or self-made binding
- 2 (½") plastic rings
- Powder blush and cotton swab
- Black fine-point permanent marker
- Basic sewing supplies and tools

Instructions

Quilt

Step 1. From blue fabric cut one rectangle 6" x 9", two strips each 1¾" x 11" and 1¾" x 10½". From gold fabric cut two strips each 1½" x 9" and 1½" x 8".

Step 2. Trace appliqué pieces onto paper side of fusible transfer web; cut out leaving roughly ½" margin around shapes.

Step 3. Fuse appliqué pieces to wrong side of selected fabrics according to manufacturer's directions; cut out on tracing lines.

Step 4. Referring to photo, position appliqué pieces on blue rectangle; fuse in place.

Step 5. Pin or baste fabric stabilizer to back of blue rectangle. With matching rayon embroidery thread in needle and all-purpose thread in bobbin, satin-stitch around each piece except stars, beginning with background pieces and working toward the foreground. Trim threads and remove stabilizer.

Step 6. Referring to photo, draw eyes, hair and mouth with black fine-point permanent marker. Make cheeks with powder blush and cotton swab.

Step 7. Stitch longer gold strips to top and bottom of block and shorter gold strips to sides. Press toward blue. Repeat with blue strips.

Step 8. Cut muslin backing and batting 12" x 15". Sandwich batting between fabric layers and baste. Machine-quilt around angels and heart and in the ditch along seams. Use machine-quilting thread in needle and all-purpose thread in bobbin.

Step 9. Bind to finish. Sew plastic rings near top corners for hanging.

Stocking

Step 1. Using stocking pattern, cut front from blue print and back from muslin.

Step 2. Prepare appliqué pieces as in Steps 2 and 3 above.

Step 3. Referring to photo, position heel and toe and appliqué pieces on stocking; fuse in place. Fuse stocking cuff to top of stocking, matching top edges.

Step 4. Machine-appliqué and draw faces as in Steps 5 and 6 above.

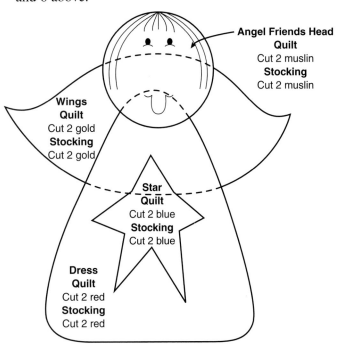

Angel Friends Head
Quilt
Cut 2 muslin
Stocking
Cut 2 muslin

Wings
Quilt
Cut 2 gold
Stocking
Cut 2 gold

Star
Quilt
Cut 2 blue
Stocking
Cut 2 blue

Dress
Quilt
Cut 2 red
Stocking
Cut 2 red

Step 5. Position stocking front and back wrong sides together and stitch with ¼" seam around curved edges. Clip curves and turn right side out; press.

Step 6. Cut a blue strip 2¼" x 11". Fold in half lengthwise and press. Press one end of strip under ¼". Place raw edges of strip together with top edge of stocking.

Beginning 1" from pressed-under end of strip, sew to top of stocking. Place raw end of strip inside pressed end. Stitch in place. Finish seam of band with zigzag stitch; press.

Step 7. Cut blue strip 1¾" x 6". Fold long edges in ⅜" to center of strip; press. Bring folded edges together again; press and stitch along folded edges. Fold loop in half and finish raw ends with zigzag stitch. Position loop inside left top corner. Stitch bottom edges to back of stocking.

—*By Angie Wilhite*

Stocking Pattern
Enlarge 150% for full-sized pattern

**Angel Friends
Heart
Quilt**
Cut 1 red
Stocking
Cut 3 red

**Angel Friends Stocking
Cuff**
Cut 1 gold

**Angel Friends Stocking
Toe**
Cut 1 gold

**Angel Friends Stocking
Heel**
Cut 1 gold

Star Tree Skirt

Have you ever considered the gift of a Christmas tree skirt for newlyweds? Collecting and building Christmas traditions is exciting in a new household.

Project Specifications

Skill Level: Intermediate

Tree Skirt Size: Approximately 48" x 48"

Materials

- 2½ yards cream-on-cream background fabric
- ½ yard red-and-green Christmas print
- ½ yard each red and green print
- 7 yards red piping
- 2⅔ yards backing fabric
- 2⅔ yards polyester fleece
- 26" x 20" piece of paper
- All-purpose thread to blend with fabrics
- 1 spool natural quilting thread

Instructions

Step 1. Fold paper in half lengthwise. Measure a 24" line along fold. Mark point of intersection 12" from point A and 20" from point B. Draw connecting lines from marked intersection to points A and B. Cut folded paper along these lines; open to form pattern piece (see Fig. 1).

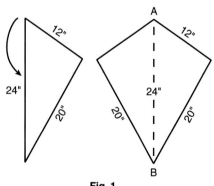

Fig. 1

Step 2. Using pattern piece created in Step 1, trace and cut six panels from cream-on-cream background fabric.

Step 3. Cut 2" strips across width of red, green and Christmas prints.

Step 4. With right sides together and using a ¼" seam, sew a Christmas print strip to one diagonal edge of each panel as shown in Fig. 2. Cut off excess

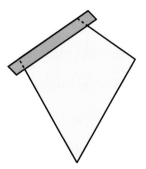

Fig. 2
Sew print strip to one diagonal side of panel.

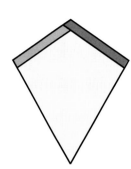

Fig. 3
Sew red strip along remaining diagonal side of panel.

fabric at same angle as panel. Press seam allowance toward strip.

Step 5. Sew a red strip along remaining diagonal side of each panel as shown in Fig. 3. Trim and press as in Step 4.

Step 6. Continue to add strips to complete each panel as shown in Fig. 4.

Step 7. Sew all panels together except last two sides as shown in Fig. 5.

Fig. 4
Continue to add strips as shown.

Step 8. Sew piping to two open sides and around all outside edges, clipping to turn corners.

Step 9. Fold tree skirt in half to use as pattern. Open backing fabric and fleece to full width. Place fold of skirt along straight edge. Cut out one half of lining and fleece at a time.

Step 10. Sew two lining pieces together only to center.

Step 11. Cut a 3" hole at the center of skirt, fleece and lining. Layer right sides together; pin or baste. Stitch around outside edge, leaving opening for turning.

Step 12. Turn right side out, close opening and press. Stitch in ditch to hold layers together.

—By Sandy Garrett

Fig. 5
Sew panels together,
leaving two sides open
as shown.

The Night Before Christmas Gift Exchange

Snowflake Angel Ornament

*As quick as the flurry of wings, sew up a flock of sweet Christmas angels
to give to your special friends for trimming their Christmas trees and wreaths.*

Project Specifications

Skill Level: Beginner
Ornament Size: Approximately 4¾" x 4¾"

Materials

For each angel
- Fabric scraps for dress and apron
- Small crocheted doily
- Preprinted button face
- Fusible transfer web
- Extra-heavy fabric stabilizer
- Polyester fiberfill
- Doll hair
- All-purpose thread to blend with fabrics
- Gold or silver ⅛"-wide ribbon
- Gold or silver metallic embroidery floss
- Heart craft paper punch
- Fabric adhesive
- Black extra-fine-point permanent marker
- Basic sewing supplies

Instructions

Step 1. Trace dress pattern on wrong side of one piece of dress fabric. Place two pieces of fabric right sides together and stitch directly on tracing line around entire pattern. Trim around stitches and clip curves.

Step 2. Cut small slit near top of backside of dress. Turn dress right side out through slit.

Step 3. Trace apron pattern on paper side of fusible transfer web; cut out leaving roughly ½" margin around shape.

Step 4. Fuse to wrong side of apron fabric according to manufacturer's directions. Cut out on tracing line. Center on dress and fuse.

Step 5. Trace wing pattern on extra-heavy fabric stabilizer. Cut out on tracing line.

Step 6. Lightly stuff dress with polyester fiberfill.

Step 7. With 2 strands of gold or silver metallic embroidery floss, buttonhole-stitch around wings. Punch wings with heart punch as shown on pattern piece.

Step 8. With fabric adhesive, glue crocheted doily to apron, button face to top of dress, wings to back of dress and hair to button face.

Step 9. Form loop with 7" piece of metallic ribbon and glue between head and wings for hanger. Form hair bow from ribbon and glue as desired.

Step 10. With black extra-fine-point permanent marker, draw freckles and other facial features as desired. Vary angel dresses, hair and crocheted doilies to personalize each ornament.

—By Leslie Hartsock

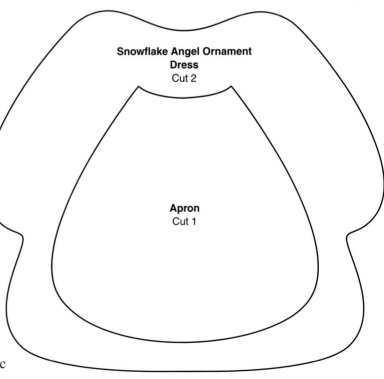

Snowflake Angel Ornament
Dress
Cut 2

Apron
Cut 1

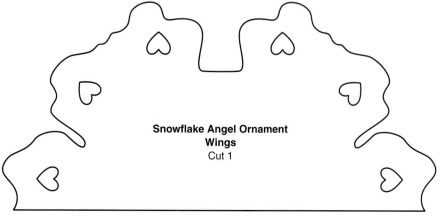

Snowflake Angel Ornament
Wings
Cut 1

Christmas Denim Shirt

Anyone on your gift list will be delighted to receive this bright holiday theme shirt—especially knowing it was personally handcrafted by you!

Project Specifications

Skill Level: Beginner

Shirt Size: All sizes

Materials

- Long sleeve denim shirt
- Scraps of red, green, blue and yellow fabric for appliqué
- Scraps of fusible transfer web
- 5 (⅝") star buttons, 4 (½") round wooden buttons and 23 assorted small buttons
- Red rayon machine-embroidery thread
- All-purpose threads to match fabrics
- Black machine-quilting thread or 6-strand embroidery floss for buttonhole stitch
- 8" (⅜"-wide) red satin ribbon
- Basic sewing supplies

Instructions

Step 1. Prewash shirt and fabrics.

Step 2. Trace appliqué shapes onto paper side of fusible transfer web; cut out leaving roughly ½" margin around shapes.

Step 3. Fuse to wrong side of selected fabrics according to manufacturer's directions; cut out on tracing line.

Step 4. Position appliqué pieces, referring to photo as a general guide; fuse in place.

Step 5. By hand or machine, buttonhole-stitch around each appliqué piece.

Step 6. With red machine-embroidery thread, use a decorative-heart stitch to sew a border down each side of the front placket and around collar and cuffs. Satin-stitch a line connecting the mittens.

Step 7. Referring to photo as a general guide, sew decorative buttons in place with doubled all-purpose thread.

Step 8. Tie a small bow with satin ribbon. Stitch to mitten string as shown in photo.

—By Michele Crawford

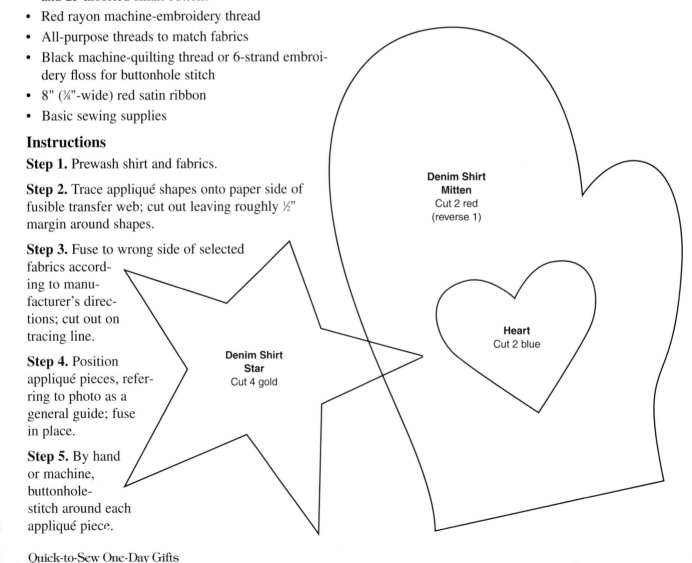

Denim Shirt Mitten
Cut 2 red
(reverse 1)

Heart
Cut 2 blue

Denim Shirt Star
Cut 4 gold

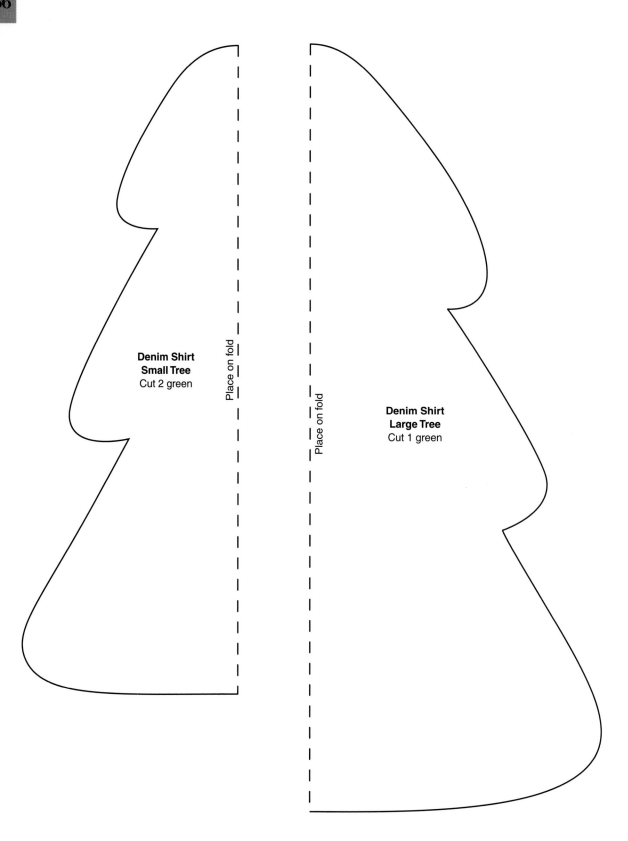

**Denim Shirt
Small Tree**
Cut 2 green

Place on fold

Place on fold

**Denim Shirt
Large Tree**
Cut 1 green

Pet Stockings

When the stockings are hung by the chimney with care, be sure everyone is remembered with a personalized stocking—even your fine furry friends.

Project Specifications

Skill Level: Beginner

Stocking Size: Approximately 10½" x 12"

Materials

For Border Print Stocking

- ⅓ yard border print fabric
- 3 (¾") black velvet-covered buttons
- 1½ yards black piping

For Bandanna Jingle Stocking

- ⅓ yard dog or cat print fabric
- ¾ yard red bandanna print
- 4 large and 4 small red jingle bells

For Colorful Striped Stocking

- ⅓ yard animal print fabric
- ¾ yard black-and-white check fabric
- 1½ yards red piping
- Scraps of 2 red prints
- 3" red tassel

For each stocking

- ⅓ yard coordinating lining fabric
- 14" x 24" fusible fleece
- All-purpose thread to match fabrics
- Chalk marker
- Wooden spoon
- Ruler
- Basic sewing supplies and tools

Instructions

Border Print Stocking

Step 1. Trace stocking pattern (enlarge as directed) on page 159 adding ½" seam allowance.

Step 2. Cut stocking front, positioning as desired on border print. Reverse pattern and cut stocking back. Cut two (reverse one) from lining fabric. Cut two (reverse one) from fusible fleece, ½" smaller than stocking all around.

Step 3. Center fleece on wrong side of stocking fabric, front and back; bond in place following manufacturer's directions.

Step 4. Stitch piping around stocking front, but not across

top. Place right sides of stocking together. Stitch around periphery, leaving top open. Clip curves; press seams.

Step 5. Stitch piping around top of stocking.

Step 6. Cut scrap of fabric 4" x 10" for hanger. With right sides together, fold in half lengthwise. Stitch a ¼" seam. Turn right side out; press. Fold in half, matching raw edges. Position at top of stocking, loop toward the heel. Stitch close to edge through all layers to secure.

Step 7. Place lining pieces right sides together. Stitch, leaving top open, clip curves and press. Place stocking inside lining, right sides together. Stitch around top, leaving opening for turning.

Step 8. Turn right side out through opening. Use wooden spoon to position lining inside stocking. Tack lining in place through all layers at toe and heel.

Step 9. Stitch buttons in place, referring to photo.

Bandanna Jingle Stocking

Step 1. Trace stocking pattern (enlarge as directed) on page 159 adding ½" seam allowance.

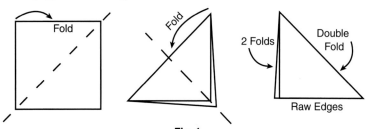

Fig. 1
Fold squares three times as shown to make prairie points.

Step 2. Cut eight 2½" squares of bandanna fabric. Fold in prairie points as shown in Fig. 1. Press well.

Step 3. Cut stocking front from animal print. Reverse pattern and cut stocking back. Cut heels and toes as directed on templates.

Step 4. Place toe piece on matching stocking piece, right sides together as shown in Fig. 2. Stitch with ¼" seam

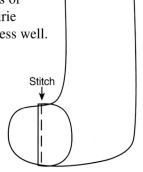

Fig. 2
Position toe piece on stocking as shown and stitch.

allowance. Flip piece toward toe; press and trim to match stocking. Repeat with remaining toe.

Step 5. Stitch heel in place on front and back, as in Step 4.

Step 6. Cut two pieces (reverse 1) fusible fleece, ½" smaller than pattern all around. Center fleece on wrong side of stocking fabric, front and back; bond in place following manufacturer's directions.

Step 7. Draw horizontal line 3" from top of stocking front and back with ruler and chalk marker. Position raw edges of four prairie points along each line, tucking one inside another as shown in Fig. 3. Stitch across raw edges to hold in place.

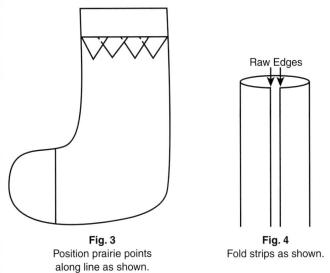

Fig. 3
Position prairie points along line as shown.

Fig. 4
Fold strips as shown.

Raw Edges

Step 8. Cut two strips 2" x 8" from bandanna fabric. Fold, wrong sides together as shown in Fig. 4. Press. Place one strip over each row of prairie points. Topstitch close to each edge.

Step 9. Place right sides of stocking front and back together. Stitch around periphery with ½" seam allowance, leaving top open. Clip curves; press seam open. Turn right side out.

Step 10. Cut scrap of fabric 4" x 10" for hanger. Right sides together, fold in half lengthwise. Stitch a ¼" seam. Turn right side out; press. Fold in half again, press and stitch close to edges. Fold in half to make a loop, matching raw edges. Position at top of stocking, loop toward the heel. Stitch close to edge through all layers to secure.

Step 11. Cut two stockings from lining fabric, reversing one. Place right sides together and stitch around outside, leaving top open and opening in back for turning. Clip seams; press.

Step 12. Place stocking inside lining, right sides togeth-

er. Stitch around top with ½" seam allowance. Turn right side out through opening in lining. Close opening. Use wooden spoon to position lining inside stocking. Tack lining in place through all layers at toe and heel.

Step 13. Stitch one jingle bell on the tip of each prairie point, alternating large and small bells.

Colorful Striped Stocking

Step 1. Trace stocking pattern (enlarge as directed) on page 159 adding ½" seam allowance.

Step 2. Cut a 5" square from checked fabric. Cut in half diagonally to make a triangle as shown in Fig. 5. Cut 3" strips of each fabric and strip-piece along edge of triangle to create pieced fabric sheet 19" square as shown in Fig. 6, using other triangle to complete square. Press seams in one direction.

Fig. 5
Cut triangle as shown.

Step 3. Cut two stockings from stripped piece, reversing one, as shown in Fig. 7. Cut two stockings from lining fabric, reversing one. Cut two pieces from fleece, reversing one, ½" smaller all around.

Step 4. Center fleece on wrong side of stocking pieces and bond following manufacturer's directions.

Step 5. Stitch piping around front of stocking (not across top). Place stocking pieces right sides together and stitch around periphery (not across top). Repeat with lining.

Step 6. Place lining inside stocking, wrong sides together. Position with wooden spoon. Baste around top close to raw edges.

Step 7. Cut two cuffs on fold from checked fabric. Fold, right sides together and stitch ½" center back seam. Repeat with other cuff. Place cuffs together, wrong sides facing. Stitch close to long edge at top. Bind lower edges together with 2½" strips of one fabric cut on the bias.

Step 8. Slip cuff over stocking with back seams matching. Stitch in place with ¼" seam allowance. Bind raw edges with bias binding.

Step 9. Cut scrap of fabric 4" x 10" for hanger. Right sides together, fold in half lengthwise. Stitch a ¼" seam. Turn right side out; press. Fold in half again; press. Open folds and turn under ½" on one short edge; refold long edges and stitch close to edge. Fold in a loop; position inside cuff at back seam with finished end on top. Hand-stitch in place.

Step 10. Attach tassel to point of cuff.

—By Beth Wheeler

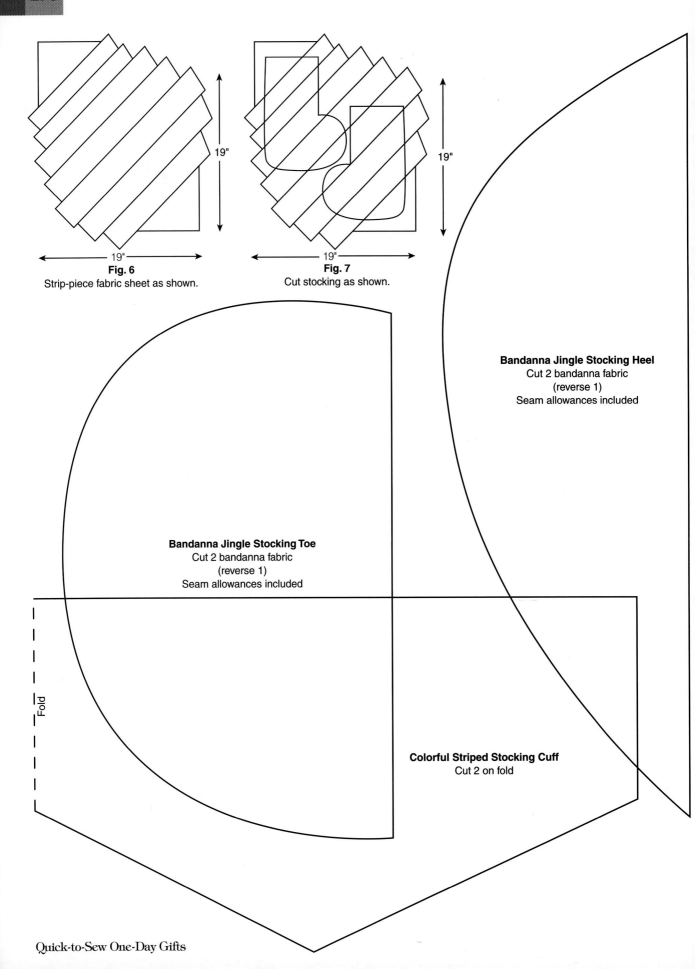

Fig. 6
Strip-piece fabric sheet as shown.

19"

19"

Fig. 7
Cut stocking as shown.

19"

19"

Bandanna Jingle Stocking Heel
Cut 2 bandanna fabric
(reverse 1)
Seam allowances included

Bandanna Jingle Stocking Toe
Cut 2 bandanna fabric
(reverse 1)
Seam allowances included

Fold

Colorful Striped Stocking Cuff
Cut 2 on fold

Santa Place Mat Set

Christmas morning is such a festive time! Children, and big kids, too, love seeing the holiday theme carried throughout the house—especially when it's Santa!

Project Specifications

Skill Level: Intermediate
Place Mat Size: 18" x 12"
Napkin Size: 17½" x 17½"

Materials

For each place mat/napkin set

- 18½" x 18½" square red print for napkin
- ⅜ yard green print for place mat
- Scraps of muslin (face), red, black, white and yellow for appliqué
- Scraps of fusible transfer web
- Fleece 12½" x 18½"
- 1½ yards purchased or self-made bias binding
- Machine-embroidery thread to match appliqué pieces
- All-purpose thread to match fabrics
- Red and black 6-strand embroidery floss
- Gold metallic thread
- 1 spool matching or contrasting machine-quilting thread

Instructions

Step 1. Finish napkins by folding edges under ¼" twice; topstitch.

Step 2. For place mat, cut two rectangles 12½" x 18½" from green print.

Step 3. Place fleece between wrong sides of green print rectangles. Use a saucer as a pattern to trace a curve at each corner. Cut on the curved line to make an oval.

Step 4. Pin layers together and machine-quilt in a random pattern.

Step 5. Trace appliqué shapes onto paper side of fusible transfer web; cut out, leaving roughly ½" margin around shapes.

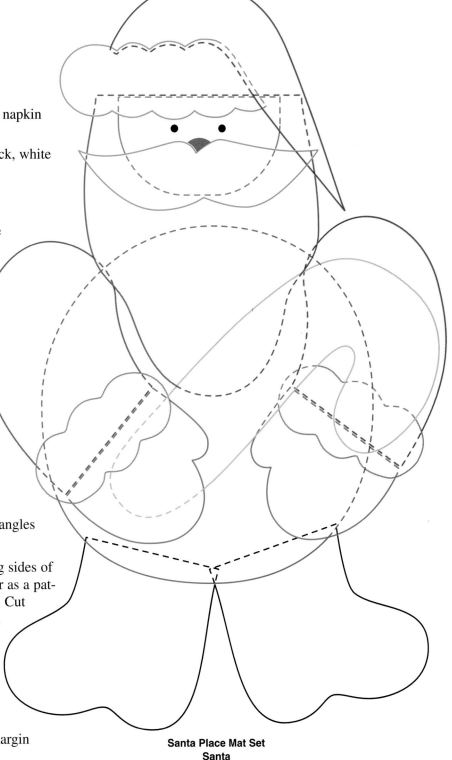

Santa Place Mat Set
Santa

Step 6. Fuse to wrong side of selected fabrics; cut out on tracing line.

Step 7. Position pieces in order, working from background to foreground of Santa. Fuse in place.

Step 8. Using matching machine-embroidery thread, satin-stitch around shapes, using photo as a guide.

Step 9. Using 2 strands of black embroidery floss, make a French knot for each eye. With 2 strands of red embroidery floss, satin-stitch a nose. With gold metallic thread, stitch a star tassel on Santa's cap.

Step 10. Topstitch around outside of mat ⅛" from edge. Bind to finish.

—By Michele Crawford

**Santa Place Mat Set
Small Star**
Cut 3 gold

**Santa Place Mat Set
Large Star**
Cut 2 gold

Basic Instructions

Basic Sewing Supplies

- Sewing machine
- Sharp scissors or shears
- Straight pins
- Hand-sewing needles
- Thimble (optional)
- Seam ripper
- Chalk marker or fade-out pen (for temporary marks)

An iron and ironing board, although not strictly sewing tools, are essential to great-looking projects. Don't be afraid to use them liberally!

Handmade Stitches

Buttonhole Stitch

(Sometimes called blanket stitch)

Working left to right, bring needle up at A, down at B and up at C with thread below needle. Stitches should be evenly spaced and of a consistent depth.

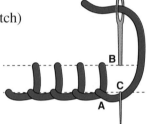

French Knot

Bring the needle up through the fabric. Point the needle at yourself, then wrap the thread or floss clockwise around the needle. Insert the needle back down through the fabric one thread away from the exit point.

Lazy-Daisy Stitch

Bring needle up through fabric at A, make a loop and hold it with your thumb. Insert the needle back down through fabric at A and up at B. Make a small anchor stitch to hold the loop in place.

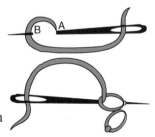

Slip-Stitch

Slip-stitching is worked by hand to make an almost invisible finish.

1. Work with a single thread along two folded edges.
2. Insert needle in one fold and slide a short distance.
3. Pick up a thread from the other folded edge and slip point of needle back in first fold.

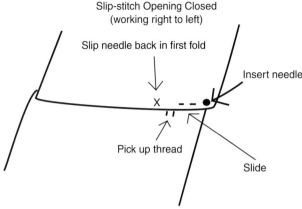

Slip-stitch Opening Closed
(working right to left)

Slip needle back in first fold

Insert needle

X

Pick up thread

Slide

4. Repeat (slide, pick up thread, insert back in first fold) along length of opening.
5. Bury knot between folds.

Straight Stitch

The basis of many hand-embroidery stitches, the straight stitch is formed by bringing the needle up at A and down at B.

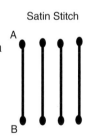

Straight Stitch

A   B

Satin Stitch

Satin stitches are simply straight stitches worked very closely together to fill in a solid shape. That shape is sometimes outlined for additional definition. ***Note: threads should lie closely side by side, but not overlapping.***

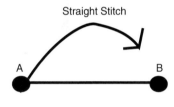

Satin Stitch

A

B

Enlarging Patterns

There are several ways to enlarge patterns—all of which are perfectly acceptable. Please choose the method that works best for you.

Photocopy

Photocopy the pattern provided at a copy shop at the percentage enlargement you want (100 percent is the size of the original; 150 percent is 1½ times the original; 200 percent is twice the size of the original, etc). If the shopkeeper objects, due to copyright infringement, tell him you have permission from the publisher to make one copy so you don't have to cut the book (show him this note, if necessary).

Grid Pattern

Any pattern can also be enlarged using a grid pattern.

The printed pattern will most likely have a grid drawn on it already. If not, draw a grid on the pattern every ½". Then, draw 1" grid on a piece of tracing paper or other lightweight paper. The final step is to transfer the lines in each grid from the pattern to the 1" grid. This is equal to photocopying the pattern at 200 percent.

Transferring Patterns

There are several methods for transferring pattern outlines and details. Choose the one that works best for your project.

Outline Pattern

1. Place tracing paper over pattern in book or magazine.
2. Trace with pencil; cut out with scissors.
3. Place pattern on the project. Pin in place, then cut or draw around the periphery.

Graphite Paper

When details need to be transferred as well as the pattern outline:

1. Place tracing paper over pattern in book or magazine.
2. Trace with pencil, but do not cut out.
3. Place pattern on the project; insert graphite or transfer paper between the project and pattern with the media side toward the fabric.
4. Retrace design lines with a dried-out ballpoint pen to transfer lines to fabric.

Iron-on Transfer Pencil

Another method for transferring pattern details:

1. Place tracing paper over pattern in book or magazine.
2. Trace with pencil, but do not cut out.
3. Turn paper over; trace detail lines with an iron-on transfer pencil.
4. Place pattern on the project with the media side toward the fabric.
5. Apply heat with an iron, following manufacturer's directions to transfer marks to fabric.

Satin Stitch by Machine

Machine-made satin stitches are often used to finish appliqué pieces and consists of closely worked zig-zag stitches.

Stitch Size

The width and length of the stitches are determined by the size of the appliqué and the body of the fabric.

1. Small appliqué pieces call for narrow zigzag stitches.
2. Large appliqué pieces call for wider zigzag stitches.

3. Fragile or brittle fabrics, such as metallics, lamés, sheer organza, etc., require longer stitches to prevent damaging fibers and effectively "cutting" the appliqué piece out of the background.
4. Fuzzy fabrics, such as shaggy felt or synthetic fur, require wider stitches and a medium width.

Threads

Threads used for satin-stitch appliqué are chosen for their weight, color and finish.

1. For fine fabrics, those with small woven threads, choose a fine thread, such as silk, rayon, or thin cotton. Machine embroidery threads are a good choice.
2. For medium-weight fabrics, a medium-weight rayon or cotton thread works nicely. Threads in variegated colors add interest.
3. Heavy-weight fabrics might do well with a heavy-duty thread worked in a buttonhole stitch, rather than satin stitch.
4. Test threads of different weights and finishes on a sample of the fabrics in your project before making the final choice.
5. Select threads in coordinating or contrasting colors, as desired.

Helpful Tips

1. Thread upper machine with rayon thread and bobbin with a cotton or cotton-wrapped polyester thread in a thread neutral to the backing, if the back will show. Or, chose a cotton or cotton-wrapped polyester thread in the same color used on the top if the backing will not be visible in the completed project.
2. Loosen the top tension slightly. This pulls the loop of the stitch to the back for a smooth look on the top.
3. When turning inside corners, stop with the needle down in the fabric on the inside (see Fig. 1).

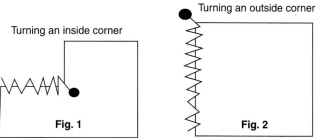

Turning an inside corner

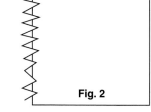

Turning an outside corner

Fig. 1

Fig. 2

4. When turning outside corners, stop with the needle down in the fabric on the outside (see Fig. 2).
5. If the machine is skipping stitches:
   - Clean the machine thoroughly, removing any build-up of fuzz beneath the feed dogs.

- Use a new needle.
- Try a needle of a different size.
- Match size and point of needle to the thread and fabric in the project.
- Apply a silicone needle lubricant to the needle, thread, and every place the thread touches the machine in the upper threading track.

6. An iron-on, tear-away stabilizer seems like an unnecessary purchase, but what it adds to the quality of a machine-appliquéd project cannot be denied. The product is ironed on the wrong side of the fabric under the area to be appliquéd. This keeps it from shifting during machine-stitching. When the work is done, the stabilizer is simply torn away. A touch of the iron adds the finishing touch for an appliqué project free of lumps and bumps!

Tea-Dying Fabric

Fabric can be dyed in a bath of strong tea to give it an aged effect.

1. Wet the fabric in clear water; squeeze excess moisture from fabric, but do not wring or twist.
2. Immerse in a hot bath of water and several tea bags. Allow to soak for 20–30 minutes.
3. Remove fabric; squeeze excess moisture out.
4. Hang fabric to dry, or dry in dryer.

Helpful Tips

- Fabric will dry lighter than it appears when wet.
- Conservationists warn that tannic acid in such a tea bath will cause damage to fabrics over a period of years, so this method should not be used on an heirloom project.
- 100-percent cotton muslin or broadcloth works best.

Gathering Stitches by Hand

Work a long running stitch close to the edge of the piece to be gathered with a doubled thread. Pull gently to gather. If fabric is heavy, use heavy-duty thread, such as carpet thread.

Gathering Stitches by Machine

To work gathering stitches by machine, set the sewing machine for the longest stitch possible (some newer machines have a built-in basting stitch). Pull the bobbin thread firmly and evenly to gather.

If the fabric is heavy, work a medium zigzag stitch over a strand of thin crochet thread. Then, pull the crochet thread to gather.

Topstitching Trims by Machine

Rickrack

To attach narrow rickrack by machine, run a straight stitch down the center of the trim. To attach wide rickrack, work a zigzag stitch or a broken zigzag along length of the trim.

Piping

To attach piping, baste close to the piping (use a zipper foot, if necessary) on one piece of the project with raw edges even. Place the other piece on the project, with right sides together, and stitch along the basting stitches through all layers of the project.

Cording

To attach cording or other narrow trims, work a zigzag stitch slightly wider than the trim with monofilament thread (for an invisible stitch) or with decorative threads for an embellished look.

Using Fusible Web

There is more than one kind of fusible web! The light or ultra-light versions have less adhesive on them and will accept machine stitches. The heavy-duty versions have a thicker layer of adhesive and are designed to be used without machine stitches. In fact, if you try to sew through the heavy-duty kind, the adhesive gums up the needle and causes a mess.

The best advice is to read the manufacturer's directions. Each manufacturer has a different formula for the adhesive and may require different handling.

Regardless of the type fusible product you choose, they may all be applied to fabric in generally the same way.

Fusible Appliqué

1. Trace the desired motif on paper side of the adhesive with a marking tool (pen, pencil, permanent marker, etc.).
2. Cut out around the marks, leaving a margin.
3. Bond the fusible webbing to the wrong side of desired fabric.
4. Cut through fabric, webbing and paper backing, following the drawn shape.
5. Remove paper backing and place the shape on desired background.
6. Fuse in place, following manufacturer's directions.
7. Finish edges with machine-worked stitches or fabric paint, if desired.

Special Thanks

We would like to thank the talented designers whose work is featured in this collection.

Michele Crawford
Christmas Denim Shirt, 164
Santa Place Mat Set, 171
Angel Apron & Oven Mitts, 46
Halloween Shirt, 131
Bear Baby Set, 68

Sandy Dye
Welcome to our Roost, 62

Donna Friebertshauser
Beaded Amulet Purse, 142

Sandy Garrett
Star Tree Skirt, 160
Wheelchair Throw, 31
Holiday Pillow Covers, 38
Stadium Throw & Tote, 32
Patchwork Vest, 146

Cindy Gorder
Veggie Kitchen Set, 50
Vintage Photo Pillow, 28

Velvet Bag, 117
Leslie Hartsock
Snowflake Angel Ornament, 162
Fleecy Kitten Robe, 115
Bright Fleece Jacket, 144
Tumbling Blocks Blanket, 74

Judi Kauffman
Apple Wall Rack, 16
Floral Pillow, 30
Cabbage Rose Tote Bag, 119

Pearl L. Krush
Holly Berry Christmas, 150
Sunbonnet Sue Doorstop, 10
Honeybee Cardigan, 134

Thaea Lloyd
Floral Wall Hanging, 21

Barbara Matthiessen
Sitting Kitties, 8
Lamb Hot Water Bottle Cover, 40

Snowman Bag & Mittens, 125
Snowman Doll, 101
Karen Mead
Chair Arm Sewing Caddy, 18
Teapot Wall Quilt, 56
Memory Pillow, 29
Rooster Pillow, 34
Memory Tote Bag, 121
Purse Accessories, 128
Annie Angel Doll, 109

Kenna Prior
Hair Scrunchies, 114
Chenille/Fleece Jacket, 136
Child's Denim Coat, 140
Chenille Stick Horse, 90
Chenille Teddy Bear, 93

Debi Schmitz
Welcome Rug & Wall
    Banner, 58

Laundry Bag Bear, 81
Veleta "Sam" Stafney
Sock Angel Doll, 89
Sock Angel Ornament, 88
Shaggy Quilted Bunny, 96
Pincushion Doll, 104
Sewing Doll, 94

Beth Wheeler
Pet Stockings, 167
Huggy Bear Draft Dodger, 14
Pet Pillows, 24
Casserole Carrier, 64
Baby Bunting, 72
Dapper Diaper Bags, 76
Christening Gown, 80
Caterpillar Toy, 106

Angie Wilhite
Angel Friends, 157

Fabrics & Supplies

Page 16: *Apple Wall Rack*—Sudberry House Shaker coat rack #10101 and HTC TransWeb fusible webbing, embroidery stabilizer and quilt batting.

Page 18: *Chair Arm Sewing Caddy*—DMC Corp. embroidery floss.

Page 28: *Vintage Photo Pillow*—Plaid Enterprises Inc. Picture This transfer medium.

Page 30: *Floral Pillow*—Coats & Clark Machine Embroidery Thread, Fairfield Soft Touch pillow insert and HTC embroidery stabilizer.

Page 34: *Rooster Pillow*—DMC Corp. embroidery floss.

Page 46: *Angel Apron & Oven Mitts*—Coats & Clark Dual Duty, Rayon, Color Twist Rayon and Metallic Threads, Bias Corded Piping and Bias Tape.

Page 56: *Teapot Wall Quilt*—DMC Corp. embroidery floss.

Page 58: *Welcome Rug & Wall Banner*—Kunin Felt Co. felt and DMC Corp. pearl cotton.

Page 62: *Welcome to Our Roost*—Therm O Web HeatnBond fusible webbing and

Warm 'n Natural batting.

Page 68: *Bear Baby Set*—Coats & Clark Dual Duty, Rayon and Color Twist Rayon Threads and Baby Rickrack, Bias Tape and Bias Corded Piping and Pellon Wonder-Under fusible transfer web, Stitch-n-Tear fabric stabilizer and Quilt's Fleece.

Page 74: *Tumbling Blocks Blanket*—DMC Corp. embroidery floss and Pellon Wonder Under fusible transfer web and Stitch-n-Tear fabric stabilizer.

Page 81: *Laundry Bag Bear*—Kunin Felt Co. felt and DMC Corp. pearl cotton.

Page 88: *Sock Angel Ornament*—One & Only Creations mini-curl hair and Beacon Fabri-tac fabric glue.

Page 89: *Sock Angel Doll*—Beacon Fabri-tac fabric glue.

Page 94: *Sewing Doll*—One & Only Creations mini-curl hair.

Page 96: *Shaggy Quilted Bunny*—The Warm Co. Warm & Natural Quilt Muslin and Beacon Fabri-tac fabric glue.

Page 104: *Pincushion Doll*—One & Only Creations mini-

curl hair and Styrofoam ball.

Page 109: *Annie Angel Doll*—Offray embroidery ribbon.

Page 115: *Fleecy Kitten Robe*—Wimpole Street Creations Wedding Ring White Chenille and Pellon Wonder-Under fusible transfer web and Stitch-n-Tear fabric stabilizer.

Page 119: *Cabbage Rose Tote Bag*—Tsukineko Fabrico fabric markers, Coats & Clark All-Purchase Thread and Duncan Disappearing Ink Pen.

Page 121: *Memory Tote Bag*—DMC Corp. embroidery floss.

Page 128: *Purse Accessories*—DMC Corp. embroidery floss and Therm O Web HeatnBond fusible webbing.

Page 131: *Halloween Shirt*—Coats & Clark Dual Duty, Rayon, Color Twist Threads and Baby Rick Rack.

Page 136: *Chenille/Fleece Jacket*—The Warm Co. Warm & Natural batting and D&CC threads.

Page 144: *Bright Fleece Jacket*—Pellon fusible interfacing and LaMode buttons.

Page 150: *Holly Berry Christmas*—Steam A Seam 2 iron on fusible web.

Page 157: *Angel Friends*—Coats & Clark all-purpose, rayon embroidery and quilting threads and Pellon Wonder Under transfer web, Heavy-Duty Wonder-Under fusible transfer web, Sof-Shape fusible interfacing, Stitch-n-Tear fabric stabilizer and Quilt's Fleece.

Page 162: *Snowflake Angel Ornaments*—Wimpole Street Creations snowflake or miniature crochet assortment, Therm O Web HeatnBond adhesive, DMC Corp. metallic embroidery floss, McGill punchline heart craft punch and Beacon Fabri-tac fabric adhesive.

Page 164: *Christmas Denim Shirt*—Coats & Clark Dual Duty, Rayon, Machine Quilting & Craft, Metallic Threads.

Page 171: *Santa Place Mat Set*—Pellon Wonder-Under fusible transfer web and Quilter's Fleece, and Coats & Clark Dual Duty, Rayon, Color Twist Threads and Bias Tape.